HE WILL HEAL

HE WILL HEAL

WILLIAM SHOWALTER, D.Min.

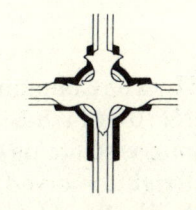

PARACLETE PRESS
ORLEANS, MASSACHUSETTS

The names, places, and many of the pertinent details in these case histories have been changed to protect the privacy of the individuals involved. The facts and the spirit remain absolutely true to life.

Copyright © 1986 by The Community of Jesus, Inc.
ISBN #: 0-941478-53-X
Library of Congress Catalog #: 86-63435
All rights reserved.
Published by Paraclete Press
Orleans, Massachusetts
Printed in the United States of America

Acknowledgements

As a man's life reflects the sum total of his friends, loved ones, and influences, so a book is crafted by a host of those who have loved, cared for, influenced, and supported the author.

I would begin that list with my wife Carol, who has loved and supported me through ministry to three congregations, years of study, and endless hours of counseling. She has walked with me through 25 years of life together, the anniversary of which, we celebrate this month. In a sense, this book is a tribute to that anniversary.

I am grateful for Cay Andersen and Judy Sorensen, who have helped me so much to see who I am, and have thus enabled me to help others. And I am grateful to the Community of Jesus, which they founded and direct, where I have found a deep love for Christ, combined with a practical working out of the Christian life, in the midst of the whole range of emotions we all experience.

My gratitude goes to the congregations who have nurtured me, and encouraged me to follow God's call to counsel — especially the members of the Parkminster Presbyterian Church, Rochester, New York, who loved me and allowed me into the deepest places of their lives, as together we discovered the enormous healing love of God.

Finally, I owe David Manuel, my editor, enormous gratitude for his skill and God-given gifts of editing and polishing this first venture in writing a book. His vision and encouragement kept me on course and committed to its completion.

William P. Showalter, D. Min.
Cape Cod

PROLOGUE		9
1	ANNE	23
2	SUSAN	35
3	RACHEL	49
4	KIRSTEN	65
5	BET	83
6	MARK	99
7	JANE	115
8	JACKIE	125
9	BETH	141
10	LOUIS	159
11	LIN	173
12	REBECCA	187
13	AMY	201
EPILOGUE		217

PROLOGUE

1. ANNE
2. SUSAN
3. RACHEL
4. HILTON
5. LIZ
6. MARK
7. JANE
8. JACKIE
9. BETH
10. LOUIS
11. LEE
12. REBECCA
13. AMY

EPILOGUE

PROLOGUE

Sometimes, after having lived in one place for a very long time, a move brings images from the past vividly to mind....

My heart was heavy, as I sat in my office on that cold, gray Saturday afternoon in November. For 17 years I had been the senior minister at Parkminster Presbyterian Church. Recently I had accepted a new call for ministry, a call that I knew was from God, and about which I was excited. But it was still a wrenching feeling to leave the place where I had served the best I could for all those years, and all those deep relationships with so many people. There had been times of suffering, as well as times of joy, and sharing them had united us with strong cords of friendship — but those cords would now be stretched and possibly broken.

I shook my head; I was supposed to be cleaning out my desk, before four young fellows from the church arrived to help pack up my books, but I kept getting lost in memories. So many years, so many friends. . . . this desk was certainly a friend. It was enormous — almost big enough to hold all the papers and stuff I had piled on it, and never neat enough to satisfy my wife Carol, who was always after me to tidy it up. It didn't do any good to explain to her that I could lay hands instantly on anything on that desk that I wanted.

My gaze wandered about the room, resting on this object or that; it was funny how important things became, when they had shared your working space for so many years. There was the plaque of appreciation, written in Spanish, and given to me by the pastors of Barquismeto, Venezuela, after we had been with them for ten days, teaching a pastoral counseling seminar. And on the ledge behind one of the twin sofas where I did most of my counseling, was an olive wood carving of Jesus bearing the Cross. And on the wall above my typewriter and dictating machine, was the first thing I saw each morning: the sacristy prayer of Martin Luther. "Thou hast made me a pastor and a teacher in the church. Thou seest how unfit I am to administer rightly this great and responsible office; and had I been without Thy aid and counsel, I would surely have ruined it all long ago. . . . Use me as Thy instrument in Thy service. Only do not Thou forsake me, for if I am left to myself, I will certainly bring it all to destruction. Amen." Every time I saw those words, I prayed them.

There was a lump in my throat, when a knock on the door sill interrupted my reverie. Looking up, I saw four smiling young men and behind them, a large assortment of empty cardboard boxes. I welcomed them and gratefully rolled up my sleeves to help, glad for something to keep my mind off of leaving.

Four hours later, it was done. The books were all packed and gone, the pictures and objects, also. I was once again alone, with just the file cabinet left, and four cartons to hold its contents. They were mostly case histories of the hundreds of people I had counseled over the years. Surely, I thought, I didn't need to save all of them; in fact, most of them I would probably never see again.

I brought the waste basket over, to receive those that didn't need to go with me — and found that I couldn't throw any of them away. These weren't files, they were people. Faces went with those manilla folders, and as I sorted through them, I looked over at the sofa, where the counselees usually sat, and I could see them, one by one, sitting there. They were usually apprehensive at first, their arms and legs tightly crossed — defensive, untrusting, taciturn.

But if there was one thing God had taught me in 17 years of counseling here, it was how to listen. . . in my heart, as well as with my ears, for any question or clue that God might give me, as to the solution of the problem. For as helpful as my academic training in pastoral counseling was, it was not the key. The key that unlocked the deepest barriers came through the intuition, not the intellect — it came from God. And so they would talk, and I would pray — for God, by His Spirit, to guide my counsel, and to intervene, touching the places where each one needed healing. For regardless of the problem, I could affirm to each one without any doubt, that God cared, and He *would* heal, in His way and in His time.

I smiled at that thought; it hadn't always been that way, with me. I had come to this church as a 38-year old pastor who had been in the ministry for 13 years, but faced a huge challenge. Parkminster was an active and growing suburban congregation with unlimited potential — the exact opposite of the one I had come from. That one had been a small, inner-city group, with blacks, Hispanics, and welfare mothers, and a scattering of professional people. Since they were obviously hurting, oppressed, and destitute, they were openly needy, and over the years we had developed a common concern for one another. And because the church was small enough, many deep and lasting friendships developed there.

So it was quite a shock to suddenly look out from the pulpit at a mass of almost faceless people, who seemed so well put together that they had no needs. It appeared that here in suburbia, everybody had moved into their new homes, to insulate and isolate themselves from others; certainly their well-groomed lawns and neatly-trimmed hedges seemed designed to do just that, and indeed, everything about their lifestyle was geared to keep people at a distance. Go to work early, arrive home late. And wives worked, as well as husbands, so no one was left home to carry on backyard conversations and develop neighborhood friendships. There was no time for anything but work, with the exception of a couple of hours on weekends with the kids. The euphemistic expression "quality time" was just coming into vogue then — mostly with parents who felt guilty about how little time they did spend with their children. Partly as a salve to the collective parental conscience, there seemed to be an endless range of organized activities for their offspring, including some at church.

Adding to my growing sense of frustration as the weeks passed, were the hundreds of people who crowded into the Sunday services, more than I had ever seen before. But the moment the services ended, they left as quickly as they had come. Going to church was apparently safe in my new parish; no one would bother you, or in any way intrude into your private space. So many people — and so many of them seemed to be newcomers.

What could the new, young pastor do to help these Christians get to know one another more than superficially? More importantly, how could I get them to even want to, let alone to really care deeply for each other? I had been studying the Book of Acts — and wishing that congregations today cared for one another, the way that the early community of believers did. Was that only possible in the first century? Or could it somehow work in 20th-century suburban Christianity?

So, summoning all my courage, I announced in the Sunday bulletin that anyone interested in a small group experience could meet on the following Saturday, in the church library at 10 o'clock. What I did not put in the bulletin was that I needed a small group myself. I was feeling lonely in this new church.

I had hoped that there might be eight or ten that would come, but I would have settled for six — enough to start with. But apparently, behind those neatly-trimmed hedges, there were other lonely people; 32 of them showed up that first Saturday. I didn't know what to do, so throwing up a fast prayer, I suggested that we go around the room and share a little about ourselves and our faith journeys. It was tentative and hesitant in the beginning, but as one after another spoke, the group seemed to gain confidence. They saw that others were exactly where they were and that it was safe to talk about such things.

Amazing — people who lived only two blocks away from one another and who had nodded to each other in church for months, discovered that their faith was equally uncertain and that both families were going through difficult times with their teenagers. That morning, a number of nodding acquaintances became friends. And their discoveries whetted their appetites for more; at the end of the meeting, they asked me if we could continue on a regular basis. And so, three Discovery Groups were born, and began meeting weekly, and there would eventually be many more.

I did not, at first, fully comprehend the dynamics of what was happening; I was just grateful that God had answered my prayer, and that I was beginning to see the seeds of the Book of Acts, taking root in our church.

People were encouraging one another in their faith and were beginning to care about one another. But as I thought and prayed about it, I began to discern God's intent for these small groups. A personal relationship with Him was the first thing that had to be established in a person's heart. But it alone was not enough; the Cross has a horizontal element, as well. A Christian was, first and foremost, to love God with all his mind and heart and strength and being. But the second Great Commandment was like unto that one: he was to care for his neighbor, as much as he cared for himself. These small groups were a gentle introduction to learning how to care.

Some problems, of course, were too personal and too deep for a small group to help, and as they surfaced, my counseling ministry took on new significance. Anyone needing private help could make an appointment and come and see me — or just drop in, if I happened to be free. My door wasn't *always* open, but I tried to keep myself as available as possible.

And on the whole, most of my daily appointments were counseling sessions.

Actually, counseling had been part of my ministry for a long time. There had been little training for it in seminary; back in the Fifties, churches were full, and psychology was not yet fashionable. We were told to preach a good sermon, teach people the right beliefs, and life would be satisfying. What I got was on-the-job training, when, as assistant minister in a rapidly growing Philadelphia church, I was given the responsibility of developing a youth program for teenagers. Gathering around me some interested and creative people, we succeeded in attracting all kinds of young people to the church, and keeping them busy while trying to impart to them the reality of the Christian life. Some of those teenagers would trust me enough to share their problems with me, and I would try to advise them, as best I could. I had not yet learned about listening to God's Spirit, and letting *Him* do the counseling, but I believe that He responded to the desire of our hearts, nonetheless. And when these young people were helped, I felt a sense of fulfillment I had not known before. I knew then, that counseling would be the aspect of my calling that I would most enjoy.

The sun broke through the late afternoon overcast, and a weak shaft of light came through the window. I cleared my throat and concentrated on the open file drawer in front of me. But it was no use; my mind seemed to have a will of its own, and what it wanted to do was reminisce. And so, with nostalgia I thought back to those carefree days before the riots of the sixties, before the drug scene, before the Vietnam war and Watergate, and before the threat of nuclear annihilation. I was single and carefree, behind the wheel of my red-orange convertible, and I liked everything about my budding call as a minister.

One day I learned that Temple University's Department of Psychiatry was offering an experimental program of pastoral counselor training in the university's medical school. Twelve ministers from Philadelphia churches would be selected to take courses and participate in psychiatric clinics with medical students. I felt a strong urge to apply for this program, and looking back, I believe that was the Holy Spirit, nudging me to embark on training which would chart the course for much of my 30 years in parish ministry.

Those first med school classes taught me things about the human personality that I never knew before, and the clinical experiences were even more intriguing. And of course, a large measure of what gripped me, was that, in the process, I was learning things that helped me understand what made *me* tick. I was still enjoying my calling a pastor, preacher and teacher, but I sensed that what I was learning would be of particular help in helping others in the future. Those two years of school flew by, and I almost regretted the day I received my Master's degree, because it meant the end of a whole new venture in my life.

I was anxious to put my newly-acquired counseling skill into practice, but God's study plan for us is often different than it would be, if we were Him. An emergency in the church thrust me into the role of senior pastor, and that took all my time and energy. Soon after, I was called to a new congregation in New England, where I met and married my wife Carol, went to the inner-city church, and then on to Rochester.

It was a big church and growing fast, and once again, there did not appear to be much time for counseling. Would I ever have the opportunity to use what I had learned? I found myself wistfully recalling those two years at Temple med school and yearning for the intellectual challenge of formal learning.

But God's schoolroom is not confined to a campus; if one pays attention in class, he comes to see that practically everything in life is either a lesson, a reward or a test. My formal training in counseling may have ended, but my real training, in His schoolroom, was only just beginning. The success of the Discovery groups brought a steady stream of people to my office, and the more I counseled, the more I learned to *listen*. And to realize how little I, with all my academic and professional training, could do to help. In fact, if I tried to offer advice in the strength of my own intellect or from the wealth of my accumulated opinions, without the guidances of the Holy Spirit, my counseling would remain on a surface level. So I prayed and listened in my heart for the still, small voice of the

Spirit, and God guided my counsel and covered my inadequacy.

He also blessed Parkminster, and several years after I came there, the church reached a place in its development, where I could at last fulfill my heart's desire and complete my formal training. With the approval of the church elders, I enrolled part-time in a doctoral program at a nearby seminary. My concentration of study was in advanced pastoral counseling, and I was blessed with several excellent professors. Here I experienced the same thirst for knowledge as at Temple, and in retrospect, I sensed that God had given me that desire, confirming that counseling was to be a significant part of my parish ministry.

The second year of my studies was spent mostly in the large mental health facility, attached to the city hospital in Rochester. Here I found myself counseling people "off the street", with greater needs than I had ever encountered in church. There were alcoholics and drug users, couples on the verge of divorce, singles so lonely and empty that they were contemplating suicide, children who had been severely traumatized and sometimes abused — desperate individuals of every type and description. Many would never be part of any Christian congregation, but they needed help as much as any member of my church.

At first, I was scared and unsure of myself, but gradually I learned to ask God for help before and throughout each session. For I had recently experienced a new, deep move of His Spirit in my life, and while my formal training had been in secular settings with secular orientation by my professors, I was beginning to appreciate how important was the supernatural aspect of counseling. I discovered that, if I kept in mind that I could do *nothing*, except pray and listen in my heart, then God, by His Spirit, would give me the key, or the insight, or the right question to ask. And as He came through, time after time, I began to trust that He would continue to do so, no matter what the situation. I was learning to lean on Him totally, and that this was the secret to effective counseling. Gradually my confidence grew, until I was willing to listen to any problem, believing that if the counselee and I both sincerely wanted God's solution, He would give it.

What I was learning now, was more profound — and more simple — than anything I had ever heard in a lecture or seen in a textbook, although much of the latter did confirm what I was learning intuitively. I was grateful for all the courses I had taken, for they had disciplined my concentration, and in the world's eyes, they were impressive. And therin lay their one pitfall: pride. Whenever I grew over-confident, and forgot to listen, or forgot that *He* was the healer, and I was merely His assistant, the results were often ineffectual. But I was learning that, too.

Again, time flew, and before I knew it, I was crossing the graduation platform to receive my doctorate. And once again, in the process of learning what affected others, I had learned more about myself. I saw how much of my past had shaped and molded me and came to a new understanding of my relationships with my mother and father. And as I began to understand why I did the things I did — especially when they were things that neither God nor I was pleased with — slowly, almost imperceptibly, by His grace I began to change.

It seemed that, no sooner was my schooling over, than my counseling load increased; indeed, it was not long before my secretary was scheduling me for five or six people a day, and often I would see several more at night. Moreover, nearly half of those whom I talked to, were not from the church, but were recommended by friends of theirs. I was working harder now, than I ever had before, and I loved it; I felt that at last I was serving God to the utmost of my ability. I thought that, with my doctorate framed on the wall behind my desk, my schooling was completed. But there was another page in God's plan of study for me.

The elders had scheduled a retreat for the weekend after I graduated. All the elders and deacons and their spouses were looking forward to spending that weekend together at a local Catholic retreat house. To lead our retreat, we had invited Cay Andersen and Judy Sorensen, the directors of the ecumenical Community of Jesus on Cape Cod, and as we gathered in the large meeting room on Friday night, I was looking forward to using my newly-acquired skills in assisting them. The room — and the whole retreat center, for that matter — contained a hushed sense of God's presence. The elders and deacons and their wives were in their seats at the appointed time, and while the atmosphere was friendly and relaxed, there was some guardedness, too, for no one had any idea how the retreat would develop.

As the meeting progressed, there was some personal sharing on the part of several retreatants. It was not deep, as people were still somewhat nervous about being there. About halfway through the evening, one of the elders who was blind got up to get a drink of water. His wife went with him to lead him safely out of the room and to the water fountain. Most of us watched this poignant scene unfold, and after they had left, Cay and Judy asked everyone to stand and for each couple to determine which was the leader in their relationship. It wasn't long before everyone was sharing about their marriage relationships, and over the next day and a half, a great amount of confession, forgiveness, healing, and deeper bonding took place between them. What the retreat leaders had done was a simple act, seemingly spontaneous, but in reality, it was led by the Spirit, and it had made all of that possible.

I was dumbfounded. Here I was, equipped with my academic degrees and much knowledge, watching two untrained women move by the Spirit lead a group into depths of honesty, reality and healing that I would never have thought possible, let alone thought of doing myself. From then on, I redoubled my efforts to let the Holy Spirit do the counseling through me. I would continue to make use of my professional training, but from that point on, if my intellect disagreed with His leading, I would go with the latter, whether or not it seemed to make any sense.

In the ensuing years, I often sought out those two women from the Community, Cay and Judy, for cumulatively their wisdom and discernment for myself surpassed any I had encountered elsewhere, and I discovered what every psychiatrist and counselor has learned: that in coming to know yourself, you prepare yourself immeasurably to help others. To the degree that you are transparent with yourself, you will be able to help others to see and know themselves.

The sun had set now, and the empty office was rapidly darkening. I switched on the desk lamp, and made a fresh attempt to get to the first file drawer. I smiled, overcome with gratitude, as I had often been in the past, that God had called me to counsel, and humbled at the thought that He had entrusted to me the care of souls. For me, there could be no greater privilege than to be used by Him to impart some word of knowledge or encouragement, or freeing word of truth, and to watch as the recipient slowly or dramatically changed into the whole person God created him to be.

I was further struck by the trust which these individuals had placed in me, sharing the most sacred and intimate moments of their lives, granting me access to the deep recesses of their hearts and souls. It was a trust that I would not violate. As I sifted through their files, in the back of my mind I was aware that perhaps one day I might want to share some of their stories in a book — one that would demonstrate the healing power of God. For I had learned through experience that He will heal *any* situation into which He is invited, no matter how seemingly hopeless, and often through the agency of a small group — neighbors in Christ, learning to love and care for one another, as they cared for and loved themselves.

But if I ever did do such a book, I would use their stories only with their approval, and even then I would take care to change their names and enough of the details of their lives, that their privacy would be preserved. If they wanted to identify themselves to their families or friends, that would be their decision; I would not bring them, or anyone in their lives, possible embarrassment.

I looked at my watch, it was past six; Carol knew I was here, and I had asked her not to wait dinner for me, but still, I had to get going. I started to sort the files. By far the largest pile were of my counselees, but there were also quite a few from the national small group program called "3D", which stood for Diet, Discipline and Discipleship. Carol had brought this program into Parkminster from the Community of Jesus, and I smiled to recall my initial reaction: I had thought of it as strictly a weight control program, a Christ-centered answer to several of the popular secular programs which required weekly weigh-ins, similar to the sort which we had already had in the church.

But soon I found that its weekly group meetings, its Biblically sound workbooks and materials and, most of all its insistence on daily prayer and caring for one another convinced me that this would be a support and assistance for those persons who needed more day-by-day care than weekly appointments with me could provide. The program grew rapidly at the church, and there there were more than 20 groups meeting each week. The ingredients of 3D worked for good in hundreds of lives, and soon it reached out across the nation, eventually touching more than half a million 3D'ers.

There was a third pile, quite a bit smaller — cases which had come to my attention from my speaking invitations around the country. As former president of the Presbyterian and Reformed Renewal Ministries, and serving in a number of other national renewal organizations, I was often called on to preach and teach at conferences and gatherings of all kinds. Frequently, I would be asked to counsel with someone else who had attended one of those meetings. Returning home, I would make careful notes of those sessions and of any follow-up that occurred, and keep the letters which would often follow.

I yawned, about to add another file to the tallest stack. I looked at the name on the file: Anne. I could see her sitting on the left sofa, and well remembered the first time she had stuck her head around the corner of my door. . . .

1

ANNE

As terrible as rejection is, fear of rejection can be even worse....

I first met Anne at the door of Parkminster Church, where I was serving as the senior pastor. It was a bright summer Sunday in Rochester, and the service had just ended. I had pronounced the benediction from the rear of the Georgian sanctuary, feeling good about my sermon and the large number of people who were at worship. I loved everything about the church — a stately brick structure, with a recently built sanctuary. Someone had done a marvelous job of decoration: the walls were a creamy off-white, the trim and wooden pews were pure white, and the carpet and wall-hanging in front were a rich burgundy.

Each Sunday, after the benediction, I stood in the narthex by the door, to greet the worshippers as they left, with my wife Carol at my side. It was an ideal time for conversation (which, I reminded Carol, had to be kept brief, for the sake of those waiting behind), and this morning I was buoyant, for I felt that the service had been endued with God's Spirit. Now, as the people came out, they were relaxed and cheerful, many of them dressed in casual summer garb.

Usually, the first to greet me were the newcomers, insecure and anxious to leave without getting involved in conversation or invited to anything. I did not hold them up, keeping our greeting short but still hoping to learn a little about them. Next would come the couples who had no children with them — faithful members whose thoughts were now on the local pancake house and the Sunday paper. Finally came the church families, having gathered up all their children from Sunday school.

About halfway through this cozy ritual, I noticed a new well-dressed couple without any children. The woman wore a lovely pink linen suit with a deep rose pin on the lapel and carried herself with a composed assurance. She was short, but there was a commanding presence about her.

Carol and I warmly greeted Anne and her husband, Brad, and learned that they had just recently moved to the city, where Brad would be the new director of a retirement home. I sensed a warm spirit about this couple, and as we briefly compared notes, to our delight we found several places where our backgrounds had intersected. When we said goodbye, I was sure that these two would be back.

They did return and soon joined the church. We were glad to have them, for they were a gifted couple. Brad had a love of music which soon involved him in the choir, while Anne was a willing, cheerful worker, assisting in church projects, wherever she was needed. She had a special talent for decoration, color, and flower arrangement and gave of herself to express God's beauty in those areas.

About a year after that first Sunday, she came and looked in at my office door. As always, she was impeccably dressed, but on this occasion, her external appearance had little to do with what was going on inside of her. "Bill," she asked, "have you got a minute?"

"Of course, come on in. In fact," I said, glancing at my appointment schedule, "I've got more than a minute; I've got almost an hour. What's the matter?"

She sat down on one of the sofas, and I sat across from her. Early on, I had learned never to counsel from behind a desk — an imposing, formidable obstacle that made the counselor seem unapproachable.

"I feel lonely and uneasy," she said, frowning, "and I have no idea why. I love being here. Brad loves his work, but —" she paused, "I don't know; I'm just — uncomfortable." We talked for awhile, as I gently asked questions about several areas of her life. On a note pad in my lap, I wrote: "Childhood?" She had volunteered very little about it. Should I ask her why? No — I got a distinct check to leave it alone, for now. Finally, as the hour ended, I suggested she consider joining a diet group called 3D that was forming in the church.

Almost six months passed before Anne sought my counsel again. She asked to talk with me about something personal, and we made an appointment for Thursday morning. This time, she seemed considerably more relaxed. "Bill, you'll never guess what's happened to me! I took your suggestion and joined 3D, and it turned out to be a great experience. I feel really close to the girls in the group — closer, I guess, than I've ever felt to any women anywhere. I've gotten a lot of help with my own life. And oh, yes," she laughed, "I also lost some weight in the process." I laughed, too; the diet aspect was what initially attracted the majority of 3D people to the program. But after they started, most of them had the same experience as Anne — finding many other areas of their lives being touched and helped, as they learned to care for each other.

"You know, come to think of it," Anne went on, "I've never been close to my peers before. I was content to sort of cling to Brad; he was more outgoing and led the way. I grew up with only one sister, and she was not around for long. In fact, Mother never talked about what happened to her." She grew pensive and frowned slightly at the thought of her sister, and I wondered if she was going to share about her childhood now. But she took a deep breath as if to catch herself from going down that path, and continued, "Well, after we had finished the first 12-week session of 3D, I was wondering whether I should join up for the second session. I really liked it, but 12 more weeks of watching what I ate seemed like too much. And then, a few days ago, I was sitting in my kitchen working on menus, when the phone rang. It was Carol."

I could picture Anne, sitting in her kitchen. Carol and I had been invited to dinner at Anne and Brad's home several times, and had become friends. The kitchen was small but very attractive, and like every room in their house, it reflected Anne's flair for color coordination and design, with everything in its place.

"Anne, are you sitting down?" Carol had asked. "You'll never dream what I'm going to ask you to do." Anne felt panic taking over. Her mind raced, as she wilted on the counter stool. She was always threatened by the slightest new venture, she told me, because she didn't feel accepted by anyone. So any new undertaking presented the possibility for failure and rejection.

Recounting the episode now, Anne was almost visibly shaking, so real was the scene to her. I was surprised; how could a person so talented and apparently so secure be so afraid of rejection? Where was that sense of rejection coming from? I still knew little of Anne's background, but I was ready to listen, as she told me of the rest of the phone conversation. "Anne," my wife had said, "we urgently need more leaders for 3D groups. More and more people are signing up, and we'll be starting several new groups. Would you pray about being a leader?"

Anne had sat stunned. Why would anyone want me to be a leader, she thought. If they knew the real me, they would never ask me to do anything. They wouldn't even want to associate with me. Yet, at the same time, she wanted to do it very much. Maybe I am worth something, after all, she mused. But immediately her mind answered her: No, Carol just called her because she couldn't find anyone else, and they were desperate.

As Anne talked, the question persisted in my mind: How had this well-dressed, alert, professional woman become so afflicted with self-doubt and fears about her acceptance? I made another note: "plagued by inner fears for a long time — why?" I understood now, why she had a hard time relating to other women, or making friends, and why she kept to herself and hid behind her husband — but what was the root?

Sitting in the early American, wing-backed chair in the the corner of my office, Anne suddenly seemed like a little girl, overwhelmed by that big chair. Seeing the hint of tears coming to her eyes, I indicated the box of kleenex on the bookshelf next to her. But she quickly regained control and ignored them.

Ask her about her childhood now, the thought came to me. "Anne," I said, as gently as possible, "would it be all right if we talked a little about your background?"

The question surprised her, and her lips tightened, but at the same time there was the slightest hint of relief in her face. She nodded, but she was moving her hand back and forth on the arm of the chair; I sensed reservation, as if she were saying, Yes, go ahead, but be careful. "Where should I start?" she asked.

I smiled. "Why don't you begin at the beginning? Take a deep breath and ask the Lord to help you."

She had been born in Bloomington, Indiana, and she could not remember much of the first five years of her life. Her mother told her they were no different from any other family, but they were living in a public housing project, and gradually that made her realize that they *were* different from other families: they were poorer.

Anne recalled one afternoon, when she was about five. She had come in from playing with some other children, and her mother was standing at the sink, peeling some potatoes for supper. One of the children had asked Anne about her father, so now she asked, "Mommy, where is my father?"

Her mother froze for a moment, then came and sat down at the kitchen table with her. She had a hard time getting the words out, and finally spoke almost in a whisper. "Dear," she said, "you don't have a father. When I was younger, I was in love with a man who already had a family. When you were born, he wanted to leave his family and be with us, but he couldn't. He was a good man, and he loved you. And I loved him very much. There was nothing I could do."

You don't have a father — Anne said that those words had haunted her all her life. Her mother had given birth to her in a Salvation Army hospital in Indianapolis, far enough away from home to avoid the shame she would have had to face. Looking back, Anne remembered that four of her mother's close friends were also women who had children but no husbands. She also recalled now, that her mother used to do volunteer work at a church-supported home for unwed mothers. That could have given her a clue, had she been old enough to put it together.

From that moment in her fifth year — and as she described it, it was obvious that she was reliving the scene — she had felt unacceptable and rejected. In first grade, every girl seemed to have a father, and many often mentioned their fathers in class. Anne was deathly afraid that someone would ask about hers. She quickly learned how to avoid being trapped into answering such a question. It was then, she believed, that she began to hold herself back and not let anyone get too close, for fear they would ask about her parents.

Several years later, Anne learned what the word "illegitimate" meant: that she had been born out of wedlock. How she hated that word and would have liked to erase it from the dictionary! Why, she wondered, did the man who fathered her, abandon her? Was something wrong with her that made the man leave her mother, before his daughter even arrived? Her mother had told her that the man loved her, but that didn't satisfy Anne or ease the pain in her heart. She was ashamed of her birth — and angry at her mother for having given her that awful start in life. It was her third-grade teacher, who finally asked her one day: "What's your daddy's name, honey?" She fumbled for an answer and really said nothing, becoming paralyzed with embarrassment in front of the other children, and full of hatred of her mother for putting her in this predicament. For years, she had carried that hatred with her, until finally, as a Christian adult, she had been able to release it to God, and forgive her mother. I made a note that, when the time was right, I would point out to her that she had much to be grateful to her mother for, because other pregnant women in her predicament had chosen the abortion route.

But not now, for at this point, Anne's words which had started so haltingly were tumbling out in a rush, as if a dam had broken, and all the pent-up feelings of all those years were finally pouring out. This was the source of her feelings of rejection and fear — the demons which had pursued her all her life.

The torment continued. As early as her primary school years, she had begun her desperate attempt to prove that she should exist, after all. Academically, she worked so hard that she made herself a straight A student. She developed all her abilities to the fullest extent, eagerly doing anything that anyone asked her to do, if it meant winning approval. And conversely, anything she did which was less than perfect, made her feel unacceptable. Any failure was devastating. It became crucial for her to be the best in everything.

This pattern continued unbroken, and as an adult, she was driven to buy the best clothes, have the best furniture, and do the best job. "I thought this would make me acceptable," Anne said wistfully, "but it never did, not in my eyes. No matter how hard I tried, or how much I succeeded, or how many nice things I bought, I did not feel acceptable. The least little imperfection would always throw me back into the pit of despair."

She developed a phobia of taking tests. She could be first in a class and know all the material, but when she sat down to take an exam — the final act of approval or disapproval, the place where her possible failure would be permanently recorded — she froze, and would wind up the course with one of the poorest grades. Nor did the situation improve, when she went away to college. As an entering freshman at Miami of Ohio, she and the other incoming students were asked to write personal histories. Anne took the maximum time allowable on the assignment, and then did a masterful piece of creative writing, as she told of her birth without mentioning her parents.

Even to this day, she sighed, her overriding fear was that she would be "found out". Someday, someone whom she cared about and was close to, would learn of her illegitimate birth and would no longer want anything to do with her. She longed for close friendships, but she had to protect her "secret", so she stayed aloof and reconciled herself to a life of isolation. Cutting herself off from others had fostered paranoia about what they were thinking of her, for she always assumed the worst. "It's been awful!" she exclaimed with great feeling.

I got up and went to the window. "Well, Anne," I said, looking out, "maybe you ought to do what Carol suggested: pray and see if God wants you to lead a 3D group. It would help you to stay focussed on the needs of others and not think of yourself so much. And it would give you an opportunity to get closer to some of the women of the church. Because at some point, you are going to have to deal with that terrible fear." I turned and looked at her. "And of course, you need God's healing for your feelings of guilt and rejection. I can help you with that, when you feel you're ready."

It had been a long and painful session for Anne, yet she did seem better at the end. Just before she left, I prayed with her, asking God to reveal to her that He loved her and accepted her.

Three weeks later, she asked for another appointment. I assumed that she was ready to work on the healing of her emotions, concerning her past, and indeed she was ebullient when she arrived. "You'll never guess what happened!" she exclaimed, almost bouncing out of the chair. "Carol probably told you: I did accept that invitation to lead a group." I nodded, recalling that Anne was on the list of new leaders that Carol had read to me. "Well, last Monday." she went on, "I went to the 3D leaders' meeting. We met in the chapel and sat around in a circle, sharing some personal concerns. I didn't want to speak, but I felt I had to, and I started to tell of my fear of leading my group. At that instant, my eye caught the gold cross on the altar, and suddenly, from out of nowhere, I heard myself blurting out, 'I'm an illegitimate child.' I couldn't believe what I had said! The secret I had guarded so closely for 40 years was out!"

She described how those dread words seemed to hang, reverberating in the air. She wanted to run out of the chapel, out of the church, and out of Rochester, all at once. But when she went to get up, she couldn't move. There was dead silence. It felt like an hour passed, and nothing happened, no one moved or said anything. She fully expected to see the 28 women there, get up and file silently out of the room.

But that was not what happened. "Suddenly," she continued, "one by one, they told me that they loved me and accepted me, just as I was. And each one came over to where I was sitting and gave me a hug. And their hugs were so warm and reassuring — the whole thing was overwhelming!" Her voice broke, and she struggled to continue. "I felt like — I was taking a bath in a pool of warm love." And now she could not go on, and was grateful for the kleenex box.

Acceptance — it blew out all her circuits, and at first she could not accept being acceptable. She said she felt like a poor little girl in a candy store whose owner had suddenly told her to take all she wanted, and she began to eat all she took, and started getting sick, because it was too much for her. After the meeting was over, she drove home in a daze. Never had she felt so close to people before! Never had she been so totally free from that awful fear of disclosure, as she felt at that moment. And the fear, the thing which had held her in bondage all her life, turned out to be a phantom! When the women learned of her illegitimate birth, they didn't reject or walk away from her; on the contrary, they drew closer to her. In a flash, she saw that, because of her drive for self-protection, she had set herself up to be rejected. The thing that she feared the most, rejection, happened to her, because she rejected others before they ever had a chance to get close to her. "How much I had missed in life, living like that!" she said, shaking her head. "But no longer — as I walked around the rooms of my home that night, I still felt bathed in the warm glow which had enveloped me in the chapel. My feet hardly touched the ground."

Go over and give her a hug, too, came the thought, and so I did. It was wonderful to see the huge load of anxiety which had been lifted from her. She still had the patterns of a lifetime to change, but wholeness in God was now an imminent possibility.

In the following months, I watched Anne gradually become freer in her relationships with others. She was able to make close friends with several of the church women, and recently she dropped me a line: "It's been several years, since that day in the chapel," she wrote. "God is still at work, to change me. Oh, I still have moments when I feel insecure, but not many. I take the hurt and anxiety to Jesus. He heals the hurt and always assures me of His love and acceptance. When I am with a friend or in a group, I can tell them my fears, and it feels okay. That's been one of the important factors in my healing: my willingness to be honest about my feelings inside. I spent so much of my life, hiding my inner feelings and presenting a good external appearance, that I still slip back into that, occasionally. But God reminds me of that, and gives me the grace to pull out of the pattern. And when I find myself striving for perfection, I tell a Christian friend, and recommit the project, or whatever it is, to God. It is still a struggle, sometimes, to let people get close to me. All my old fears rise up in me. But God reminds me of the healing I have received, and I *choose* to get close to others.

"God is continually doing new things in my life that reassure me of His love to me. Recently, while I was at a retreat at the Community of Jesus, I received the following words from the Lord, as a promise:

> Have you not seen,
> Do you not know,
> That I have not forgotten
> How you were begotten?
> In the beginning I knew
> Exactly what was best for you.
> Do not fear — My love is sufficient
> My strength will endure,
> My love for your life
> Will make you secure."

I re-read the letter — and reached for the Kleenex box. Anne was truly a walking miracle. God had used what was a handicap in her life and made it a pathway to healing and wholeness. Truly, there was no limit to the ability of God to heal His children, and I bowed my head and thanked Him.

2
SUSAN

Fear is a crippling affliction, but perfect love casts it out....

Between appointments, one summer morning, I was at my desk, gazing out the window. A group of little children were in a circle on the church's front lawn, playing tag. They were part of the vacation Bible school which was in full force. I grinned; it was one of the many good things that had happened in our church in the five years I'd been there.

I glanced at my appointment book: the next hour belonged to a woman named Susan, whom I had only met on one other occasion. She was one of the older members of the congregation who had been there for years and who had been close to my predecessor. I was not at ease around those who had been friends of Dr. King. It wasn't anything they said or did, but I was still in my early forties, and he had founded the church and been involved in the births, marriages, and deaths in many of those founding families. I did not have that same place with them and felt insecure as a result.

But Susan posed another threat to me. Several years before, she had written an angry letter to the elders, protesting the denomination's giving money to defend

Angela Davis, an alleged Marxist. She and her husband Roger had declared that they were going to leave the church. Though they hadn't removed their membership, they rarely attended services. Like many pastors, I took their leaving as personal rejection and became hurt and angry inside. So it was with less than positive anticipation that I watched the clock on my desk inch up to 11:00.

Susan was on time, and I scanned her face, to see if she was angry. If she was asking for something, I was ready to bend over backwards to grant her request. I was anxious to have a good meeting with this woman, as she would most likely report the results to the other old-timers. But her expression gave me no clue where she was coming from.

"Well, Susan," I said in my most professional manner, greeting her at the door, "how can I be of help to you?"

"Dr. Showalter," she said with great hesitation, "I don't know you very well, and I haven't been very close to the church lately, but something happened to me yesterday, and I need to tell someone." I looked at her closely, and seeing how difficult this was for her, I nodded silent encouragement. "Yesterday, I went to the doctor for my annual check-up," she went on, unconsciously gripping one hand with the other. "I hadn't felt particularly nervous, since I'd been there every year for the last seven, since I had my first cancer operation."

I had not known of the operation, and on my note pad, I made a note to ask her in the future, about her medical history. The examination, she told me, had been routine, but after it, she had asked her doctor to look at her shoulder which was giving her persistent pain. She assumed it was arthritis, and wanted him to give her some medication for it. He poked and probed with his fingers for a long time — longer than was normal. Finally, he sat down in front of her and said rather seriously, "Susan, I don't like what I feel there. Maybe you had better have a thorough x-ray. With your history, we can't be too careful. I'll have my secretary schedule an appointment with the radiologist in two days." Susan froze. Hadn't she been through enough? After seven years, she had believed that her cancer was gone. But what if it had come back? Tormented by such thoughts, she felt like a condemned person with a sentence of death over her head.

I could see the anguish in her face. Lord, what do I tell her? But nothing came to me at the moment. It was obvious that she was drained emotionally and nothing more was going to come forth. She got up to leave and then said, "When you say your prayers, Dr. Showalter, please pray for me. I have to face that radiologist tomorrow."

I suggested that we pause for a prayer right then, and simply addressing God, I asked Him to intervene and bring her help. I sensed that Susan didn't know God personally and would need others to pray for her. The next day, when I called her, she had not heard anything yet, and over the phone it sounded like she was embarrassed for having told me all that she had, and was now going to close up like a clam.

Later in the week, I visited her at home. She and Roger lived in a red barnboard condominium. She was an artist by training, and her home reflected it. As she graciously showed me through the house, I noted several of her watercolors on the walls. She had decorated her kitchen and bedroom with antique stenciling. She loved antiques, and they fit perfectly into the cozy atmosphere of her home.

She gave me a cup of coffee, and gently I asked her now about her previous cancer operation. She chose her words carefully, as she began to tell me about that traumatic episode, seven years before. She had accompanied her husband for his routine physical, the internist being a friend of theirs. After Roger's examination was over, she mentioned to the doctor that she was concerned about a dimple on her breast; it looked like a small sun with rays radiating from it. Examining her, the doctor had referred her to a surgeon immediately, whereupon Susan became extremely fearful.

She had seen the surgeon the next day, and after further examination was informed that the bump was malignant — the top of a cancerous tumor. The surgeon declared that he would have to perform a radical mastectomy as soon as possible, and in addition to removing her breast, he would have to take a large piece of skin from her leg and graft it to her chest. Also, she would probably lose a lot of movement in her arm, when he removed some of the muscles and nerves.

Susan was stunned; this was the worst thing that had ever happened in her life. She and Roger were scared — so scared that they never talked about the coming operation, until the night before she was to enter the hospital. That night in bed, she and Roger had held each other and cried and cried, and when he took her to the hospital the next morning, she was a nervous wreck. She could not control her thoughts, which always turned to death, and was unable to sleep that night. In the morning before the operation, she had to be sedated earlier than usual, to calm her nerves and control her fears.

She told me that she remembered going into the operating room without knowing whether she would live or die. When it was over, and she was released, she vowed to Roger that she would never go back there again. But the fear stayed with her, and for a long time afterward, whenever she went to bed, she wondered if she would ever wake up again. She was obsessed with the thought of her cancer, wondering if the doctor had indeed removed all the cancerous tissue.

Periodically, she would try to shake off her fear,

telling herself that thousands of women had had radical mastectomies and lived long and healthy lives. Her surgeon provided her the names of former patients to visit, and she did visit several. But she soon had to stop, because she would leave the visit totally depressed, and entering her car, would weep uncontrollably. The fear of cancer lingering in her body, haunted her for the next seven years.

Now I could understand her reaction, when the doctor seemed to indicate that she might possibly have cancer in her shoulder. The trauma and fear of her previous experience was obviously still with her. She would need prayer for healing of her mind and spirit, as well as for healing of her body.

One good thing, I noted, as I finished my coffee: Susan was much more animated and free in her conversation. Apparently, she had decided to trust me. She had answered my question about her former operation, and now she proceeded to tell me about her visit to the radiologist, a few days before. On the appointed day, she had gone to the Genesee Hospital, and after a long wait, had been shown to the x-ray room, where she exchanged her clothes for a hospital gown and stood up behind a large screen. It felt cold and clammy, as the technician pressed her bare shoulder against it. "We want a picture of the right clavicle," Dr. Black said. Susan didn't know what a clavicle was and determined to look it up in the dictionary later.

As she had told me, there had been no call the next day with the results. And after a second day with no news, she got hold of a doctor friend with some connections at the hospital, and had him check with the radiologist. Later that afternoon, he called back. "Susan, it doesn't look good. I hate to tell you this, but there appears to be a tumor in the bone, and it seems inoperable. The bone is deteriorating."

Could anything be done? Yes, radiation and chemotherapy. She asked him to tell her in all honesty what her chances were, and he said, "Truthfully, Susan, given your history, they're only about 50/50."

She was in the upstairs bedroom at the time, and when she heard those ominous words, she flopped down on the bed and wept, as wave upon wave of fear and anger swept over her. The first thing, next morning, she verified the results which she already knew unofficially. Her surgeon scheduled her for a biopsy in two weeks.

The coffee cup in her hand was trembling as she told me this, and as I said goodbye, I assured her that I would be praying for her. Then, I added, "Now call me, as soon as you get the results of the biopsy. Promise?" She nodded. "Good! You make a good cup of coffee, but I don't want to wait that long to find out."

That same evening, Susan's 3D group was to have its second meeting. Three weeks before, she had been sitting in church with a friend, when she noticed an announcement in the bulletin, about an orientation meeting for a new diet program called 3D. She needed to lose a few pounds, so she persuaded a friend to come with her. When they arrived, they were astonished to have to wait in line to get into the meeting room; they had expected to see maybe a dozen or so people there, as for most minor church functions. It must be pretty good, Susan thought to herself. But when she finally arrived at the registration table and read over the application, she began to doubt her impulse of the day before. In order to join 3D, members had to make several commitments, the first of which was that they would read the Bible daily. Susan laughed, as she later recalled this. "I didn't even know if I had a Bible, unless I could find one in the attic." Then, they had to agree to call other members of the group once a week. "What in the world would we talk about?" she had thought. The next promise was to keep track of what she ate, and follow a prescribed diet. She thought she could do that all right, since she wanted to lose weight. There were Scripture verses to memorize, but only one a week.

It was the last commitment, which gave her a problem: members had to agree to pray for others out loud in the group meetings. Susan had never done that, and as she filled out the application, she was privately sure that she never would. But she joined anyway, figuring that somehow she could get around that promise, or just drop out.

The first meeting had been scheduled for the following Monday, and as Susan's friend was late, she went alone into the church chapel, where the group was gathering. She had always liked that room which had a feeling of peace and simplicity about it. It was painted in Wedgewood blue with a deeper blue rug, and a simple altar with a brass cross on it was placed against the front wall. Some of the padded wooden chairs, which normally stood in rows, had been moved into a circle at the back of the room. There were about 12 women in the group, chatting as they waited for the two leaders to join them. Most were younger than Susan and as she walked in, one girl was saying, "How nice, your husband is a Christian, too."

Then and there, Susan decided that she did not belong in that group; in fact, she felt that her chair was outside the circle the entire meeting. The two leaders came in and started the meeting, about which she later remembered nothing, except that a couple of the women were too talkative. And what was all this "Christian" business, anyway? She didn't remember a thing about the meeting, she recalled, except that some of the women were too talkative. And what was this Christian business anyway?

She spent part of the meeting, wishing she hadn't joined and wondering if she could get her money back. The other part of the time, she worried about the coming prayer time. When it was her turn to pray, what would she ever say? But in the end she was spared; that first meeting had run a little late, and so the leaders themselves did the praying to close the meeting.

The day that I'd gone to her house for coffee, Susan was so distraught about the forthcoming biopsy that she forgot all about her 3D meeting that evening, until it was almost too late for her to attend. Well, now she had a good excuse for dropping out; no one, knowing what she was facing, could blame her for that. So she called Linda, one of the group's leaders, and explained, "I really don't need it now."

"Why?" Linda asked.

"Because I —" and Susan burst into tears. She tried to go on, but all she could do was cry.

"Close your eyes while I pray," Linda said calmly, "and listen to me."

Suddenly, as Linda was praying, Susan stopped crying; she felt as though she was listening to a long-distance call to God. Someone she hardly knew, cared for her!

When Linda finished, she asked, "Won't you reconsider, and come to the meeting tonight?"

"Yes, I will," Susan replied, adding, "only please — don't ask me to pray."

"All right," Linda responded warmly, "but when your heart starts to pound, and your throat gets dry, you'll want to share." She paused. "Just remember: it's okay to cry."

That night, Susan sat quietly through the meeting, until five minutes before it was to end, when she started growing fidgety inside. A middle-aged woman on her left was talking about the problem of her husband's snoring; across the circle, a young wife had been complaining about missing socks in the laundry. Susan shook her head; if they knew about her problem, their little troubles would seem insignificant. Suddenly, she felt her heart pounding in her chest. And before she knew what she was doing, she was telling them about her tumor and her fears. She broke down and sobbed and sobbed, trying to finish. Almost immediately, other members began to cry, too. Soon, several women came across the circle and hugged her. Then the whole group gathered around and prayed for her. Never in her entire life had she ever had anything like that happen to her. After the prayer, when she opened her eyes, she suddenly noticed that her chair had moved silently back into the circle.

The day of Susan's biopsy dawned calm and very sunny. About 9:30 that morning, Linda and Beth, the 3D leaders, arrived at her home. Mildly surprised that they had come, she offered them coffee. The two leaders sat on the sofa, and then Linda leaned forward and said, "Susan, have you ever asked Christ to come into your life?"

Susan responded the only way she knew: "I've done everything I know how to do. I've tried to help out at the church, but I guess the answer is no."

"Would you like to now?"

Susan nodded. "How do I do it?"

"Well," Linda smiled, "why don't you kneel down, and then just repeat this prayer, in your own words: Lord Jesus, I know I am a sinner and have done many things that I shouldn't have. I ask you to forgive me for these sins, and I give my life to you. Please come into my heart and be my Lord and Master, from now on."

Susan told me what happened next: "I experienced a wonderful feeling, like a lovely, tingling shower, creeping over my whole body! I knew then that I belonged to God." As Linda and Beth were leaving, Linda turned to her and said, "I really believe God is healing you."

It wasn't long before Roger came home from work, to take Susan to the hospital. He was trying to be a support for his wife, but inwardly, he was just as frightened as she was. He apparently decided that avoiding all talk about the operation was the best way to keep her mind off of the afternoon appointment.

As they entered the hospital through the large ornate lobby, Roger said to her, "Would you like to stop by the chapel and say a prayer?" She was surprised. Never before had he suggested that they pray about anything. She nodded, and they found the little room which served as a place of prayer and meditation in that large and busy hospital. Quietly they knelt before the altar, and holding hands they both prayed aloud for God's help and healing. They were simple prayers, from the hearts of two people who for the first time recognized their need of help from the God who had made them.

Checking in at the reception counter, Susan was surprised to find that she was no long fearful — not at all. In fact, she was not even nervous, when the nurse took her to the x-ray lab and injected her with barium which would highlight the areas that the surgeon wanted close-ups of. Nor was there any apprehension, as she changed into the skimpy, ill-fitting hospital gown, and got up onto the stretcher table. And watching the ceiling as she was wheeled into the operating room, all she felt was a deep sense of gratitude, for her new-found Friend who was right there with her.

Greeting her at the operating table like a reception committee, were the surgeon and his partner, a nurse, and an anesthetist. As they shifted her onto the operating table, another nurse entered, with the new x-rays which were still wet, and clipped them to a back-lit viewing glass on the wall. The surgeon went over to look at them, while the anesthetist gave her an injection to numb the area of her shoulder, from which they would take the bone sample.

"Frank," the surgeon called to his partner, "come over

here and look at this; it doesn't make any sense."

His partner joined him. "I see what you mean," he said, and then he looked at the original x-rays. "Hard to believe it's the same patient."

They waited for the x-rays to dry, so that they could have a really close look under intense light. When they did, they both shook their heads, and the surgeon muttered, "Never seen anything like it in 23 years of practice." He turned to the nurse who had brought her in and said, "You can take her back to the changing room and release her."

"*What?*" exclaimed Susan. "Will you please tell her — *me* — what's going on? Aren't you going to take a sample out of my clavicle?" She knew which bone that was now.

"No!" the surgeon responded, thoroughly perplexed. "According to these latest x-rays, the bone is clean. None of the deterioration that was there before is there now. And we're certainly not going to cut into perfectly healthy bone!"

The nurse who brought her in, smiled. "What he's saying, in his own inimitable fashion, is that you're fine. We don't know how it happened, but *something* happened — anyway, you don't have to worry about bone cancer anymore. Now let's go and tell your husband."

When she saw Roger, she didn't have to say anything; he could tell by the beam on her face that miraculously, everything was all right. She quickly changed back into her street clothes, and as they were leaving, she suddenly stopped. "Could we go back to the chapel? I want to thank God." They did, kneeling together where they had, just an hour before.

Six weeks later, at the banquet celebrating the end of the twelve-week 3D session, she sat with her friend, who had joined the group with her. When it came time for the members to share what the past twelve weeks had meant to them, Susan hesitated — and felt her friend almost push her out of her chair. She stood up and started to share the whole wonderful story, when her voice choked up, and she began to weep gentle tears of joy. Roger, who was at a table in front of her, began brushing tears from his own eyes, and soon the whole room was similarly moved. When Susan was finally able to finish her story, a holy hush settled over the room, as though everyone there was in awe at the sight of a miracle.

When she sat down, she whispered to her friend, "Why did you push me so hard to get out of my chair?"

Her friend looked at her, bewildered. "But I never touched you."

The evening ended on a perfect note, when an old friend who was a tenor in the church choir, sang: "He touched me, He touched me, and oh, the joy that floods my soul. Something happened, and now I can say, He touched me and made me whole."

It has been a dozen years now, since Susan was touched and made whole by God. Recently I talked with her, and she reported that the last time she went in for a check-up, her doctor said, "Nothing has ever happened to you since that episode has it? I still can't understand it." Susan just smiled and offered a whispered prayer of thanks to her heavenly Father.

"Bill," she said to me, as we said goodbye, "I've changed almost completely since that healing took place. I view things so differently now! I want to be open and honest with myself and others. And you know what? I find I *like* people now. My purpose in life before was to raise my family and pour myself into my children and my art. I was centered in myself and had no idea of what it meant to give. Now I try to serve God by giving myself to others. He has given me a lengthened time to live, so I see each day as His gift to me. I want to use it, as He wants me to." I just looked at her and shook my head at the miracle I was witnessing. She looked ten years younger, and all the strain and fear that was on her face that first time she came to my office, was gone. She had a new friend and companion in Jesus, and as good earthly friends as anyone could ask for. They had gone through the rough places in her life with her, and would remain close to her for the rest of her life. Their love, and His, had indeed cast out fear.

3
RACHEL

"Trust in the Lord" — it's so easy to say to someone else, and so hard to do yourself. Sometimes, when a person can't, we have to believe for them, until they can....

One Thursday morning, as I came out of my office to bring some dictation to my secretary, Diane, I noticed a young woman in her early twenties, dressed in blue jeans and a blouse, sitting in the church library. She had dark hair, and a round face, and she was obviously pregnant. Diane informed me that her name was Rachel, and though she didn't attend Parkminster Church, her landlady, whom I had counseled before, had referred her to me. When Diane introduced us, she was quiet and withdrawn. It didn't take much discernment to see that she was scared.

"Hello, Rachel," I said, motioning her to a seat on one of the sofas in the office, "what brings you here?"

There was a long silence as I watched her retreat into the corner of the sofa. Finally, she took a deep breath and made a start. "I, um — I've never talked to a minister before," she said, and it didn't look like she was going to this morning, I thought, as she lapsed back into silence. Over the years, I had learned patience in such situations. The worse thing a counselor could do was press for a response. Just wait, and let the inner pressure which had brought the counselee this far, do the rest. In Rachel's case, it soon did. The words came tumbling out. "Dr. Showalter, I need help. I'm four months pregnant, and my boyfriend wants me to have an abortion. But somehow that doesn't seem right to me, so now he has thrown me out of his apartment, and I'm living with my former landlady, Edna, and her family, whom I hardly know. It was Edna who brought me to see you."

"Well," I said, smiling, "when you feel like it, why don't you tell me what you can, and then we'll see if the situation is really as hopeless as it seems."

Gradually, she calmed down and told me her story. Rachel had grown up with a man whom she thought was her father. Once, when she was six, she was awakened in the middle of the night by her mother and father fighting. As she listened through the wall, she learned that her mother had just come home drunk, and her father was furious at her. Half asleep, she got out of bed and went in the living room, where she hugged her father's leg and said in a pleading voice, "Daddy, don't fight!"

Out of her drunken fog, her mother snapped, "That's not your real father!"

Rachel was stunned. The man whom she had idolized, and who she was sure loved her, was not her flesh and blood. She refused to believe her mother, but sadly her stepfather confirmed it. He, too, was an alcoholic, and Rachel's home life steadily deteriorated, until at nine, she went to live with her mother's parents. But they had their own problems with the bottle, and she found herself enduring constant conflict, and wondering if she would have to leave again.

"I fell all over myself trying to be helpful," she told me. "I didn't want to rock the boat, or I might not have a place to live." Her yearning for attention and acceptance was not fulfilled at home, so when she grew older, she went elsewhere to find it. By the time she was 15, Rachel was hanging out in bars, playing pool, and developing her ability to flirt and arouse men's desire. After finishing high school, she went out every night to a bar, with or without a date. But no response from men was ever sufficient; she wanted continual approval and flattery. But whenever anyone wanted to go to bed with her, she would reject him and seek other dates. Every new man she met was a challenge. At 18, she became engaged to a man whom she thought would care for her, and lived with him for two years.

Rachel soon found that one man did not provide enough attention, so she dated a number of other men, while still engaged. Her promiscuous behavior finally caused her boyfriend to break their engagement, and she went down to Florida, to try to find her stepfather, the only man who she felt ever really cared for her. Unable to locate him, she returned to Rochester and on an impulse called up an old boyfriend. When he claimed that he still loved her after all the years, she moved in with him. Three months later, she became pregnant, and he asked her to leave.

As I listened to Rachel pour out her life, I made a few notes and made sure the Kleenex was available, as tears bottled up for many years were soon running down her cheeks. Born into rejection, she had lived in it all her life, while trying to find a shred of acceptance somewhere from somebody. She tried to use men for this, but they wound up using her, taking advantage of her pathetic craving to satisfy their own lust.

She ended the painful recitation with the plea: "Can you help me?" I shook my head. "I can't. But I believe Jesus can." I paused and glanced at my note pad. Sooner or later, she was going to have to take responsibility for her own actions. But was she emotionally strong enough to do that? It could anger her or plunge her even further into despair, and any chance of helping her would be lost. I prayed and decided to risk it. "Rachel," I said, as gently as possible, "if you are going to make a new start, your first step is going to have to be taking responsibility for the fact that you are where you are." I stopped there; we had talked enough for one day, and she now had something to think about. As we said goodbye, I invited her to come back the following week.

Two weeks passed, and Rachel did not return. Had my word to her about her responsibility turned her off? On Thursday of the third week, she did call for an appointment, and as soon as she settled into the maple armchair — if she had taken the sofa, she never would have gotten up again — she let me know why she had stayed away. "I was so angry at what you said, I decided I was never coming back here again!"

I smiled. "What made you change your mind?"

"I couldn't stop thinking about that responsibility thing." She paused, not wanting to go on. "And there was something else."

I said nothing, and at length, she continued. "When you mentioned Jesus, it reminded me of something which happened in Florida."

I decided to take another risk; this could be the key: "When did you become a Christian, Rachel?"

Startled, she immediately filled up with tears. "When I was twenty, looking for my stepfather. I was looking for someone stable in my life, and I thought maybe he could help me. I really needed it, because I was doing the same things down there, drinking and stuff in bars, as I had done up here. I got a job in a fastfood place, as a waitress, working the second shift."

She smiled, then, recalling that scene. "There was something different about the two women managers of that shift; they seemed to have a glow about them. One of the managers, Sue, said to me one night, as I was finishing my work, 'Rachel, I'm going to believe for you. I know God loves you.' I almost fell off the stool at the counter where I was cleaning up. I had never met a born-again Christian, and certainly no one who cared enough about me to pray for me. A few days later, Sue led me in a prayer, and I accepted Jesus as my Saviour."

Staring at the floor, in a low voice Rachel went on to say that her promiscuous behavior didn't change all that much, after her experience with Jesus. But inside, she felt more desperate about her condition; for the first time in her life, she felt convicted that the way she was living was not right. She wanted to be different, but didn't know how to go about it. Leaving the fastfood restaurant in search of her stepfather, she had no fellowship with any other Christians, so her newfound relationship with Christ withered. For the next two years, she pushed God aside and pursued her obsession for attention.

By now Rachel was softly weeping. I was grateful for the seed of love and hope that had been placed in her heart by the two waitresses. And I sensed that right now, she was beginning her journey back to her heavenly Father's home. Our time together seemed over, so I ended with a prayer, asking God to love Rachel, protect her, and draw her to Him. And I invited her to come back the following week.

She did and was right on time for her appointment. As she talked about really wanting to make a new start in her life, it came to me that she might benefit from joining a 3D group which was just beginning. I suggested that to her, and she said she would try anything that would help her break her destructive chase for men's affection. As the group was meeting that same day, I asked Diane to take her and introduce her to the members. I knew most of the women in the group; they were church members and very caring.

The following Thursday, I could see a remarkable change in Rachel. She came into my office with a brand-new maternity top and a beautiful blue skirt. Moreover, she held her head up and looked me in the eye, when she greeted me. I commented on her apparently new clothes.

"Oh," she said, still incredulous, "would you believe one of the ladies in my group *made* this outfit for me? She actually made it on a sewing machine!" She shook her head. "Do you know, this is the first time I've worn a skirt in years. I like it! I really feel better about myself. I feel like a human being, a woman, and not just a thing." She went on to tell me that one of the group members had treated her to a permanent, and others had gathered baby clothes, in anticipation of the birth of her first child.

Then she shifted the subject, as though she wanted to get something out while she still had the courage to do so. For she had begun to see how much she wanted acceptance in her life, and she wanted to talk about it. When she realized that she had no father that she knew, Rachel had tried to get positive attention by doing well in school, but no one ever paid any attention. Although she had not been unattractive as a teenager, she never seemed to have any dates, so she had begun flirting, to make boys notice her, and that had begun the pattern which had held her in its grip for so long.

So many experiences of rejection were buried inside of Rachel that it was still extremely painful for her to talk about them. But that was precisely what she needed to do — getting it all out into the open, so that she could face it with Jesus and be healed. Each week, for the remainder of her pregnancy, she came back and was able to recall more. Then I would pray with her, and another portion of her past would be forgiven, cleansed, healed , and put forever out of mind.

One week, she was crying even before she entered the office. Taking deep gulps of air to try to calm down, she told me of a hurt she had received 13 years before. She was almost shaking as she began, and it was soon apparent that this was the deepest she had faced so far. She did not go to church as a child, but one time when she was ten, she had gone to one down the street, because one of her friends had invited her to sing with the youth choir. She went five or six times on Wednesday evenings.

One evening, the director picked her to sing a duet with an older boy, as part of the Christmas morning service. "I was thrilled!" she told me, her eyes shining. "It was the first time someone thought there was something good in me." As Christmas approached, she practiced and practiced. Her mother and grandmother promised to come to hear her sing; it would be the first time they had ever done that. Rachel started to hum a tune. "You know," she said, surprised, "I can almost remember the words, after all these years. I think it began, 'God His own doth tend and nourish. . . "

She had convinced her mother to buy her a special dress for that special day, all Christmas red with white trim, and a full skirt. She had white stockings and black shoes to go with it. Christmas morning, she got up before dawn, and scrubbed her face till the skin almost came off. Then she brushed her hair a hundred strokes, and put on her new dress. "I felt like a princess! This would be my happiest day ever. And my mother would see me and be proud," she said, smiling.

A cloud passed over her face as she struggled to continue. "I went to awake my mother and my grandparents, but I discovered they were dead drunk from a party the night before. I tried as hard as I could to get them up, but they only got angry and yelled at me. No one would go to church with me. I was so hurt and rejected, that I didn't go either. I went into a corner of my room, curled up in a ball, still in my new dress, and cried and cried!"

As Rachel recounted this part, she actually seemed to become that little girl again, curling up in the chair, her shoulders heaving with deep sobs. It was as though she had lanced a long-festering boil, and all the infection and poison was pouring out. Not saying anything, I got up from the sofa and went to stand behind her chair. I put a hand on her head and prayed, "Jesus, You are not limited by time and space. Walk back into Rachel's life right now, to the time when she was in her house on that Christmas morning, long ago. Stand beside her, as she realizes that her mother is not going to go with her to church. Take her in Your arms and assure her that You love and care for her. And heal her of the deep hurt and the painful memories of that day, in Your powerful and loving name I ask it, amen."

As I prayed, I could feel the tension easing from Rachel, as she seemed to relax and accept the arms of Jesus. In a few moments, she began to softly sing her Christmas song again, as if lost in thought.

> God His own doth tend and nourish,
> In His holy courts they flourish,
> From all evil things He spares them,
> In His mighty arms He bears them.

I went back to the sofa, and when she finished, she looked at me and brightened. "You know, I haven't thought of that song in years, and if you had asked me yesterday, I don't think I would have remembered it at all, and certainly not all the words! I guess I buried it and covered it over. Can you imagine that teeny weeny seed, planted all the way back when I was ten? It survived everything, and began to grow, more than 12 years later." I nodded and smiled. In the midst of all the weeds and rocky places in her life, God had tended that seed. What she had sung was true: He had carried her in His mighty arms and protected her from the destruction of her soul.

In the last few weeks before her delivery, she opened up more and more, like a bud rose coming to bloom. She began to share her innermost feelings now, and often I did no more than listen to her, as much time was spent with the catharsis of her crying and sharing.

Rachel's 3D group met just before our scheduled appointments, and as the weeks progressed, I could see the positive effect the group was having on her, helping her to see herself differently and giving her real hope for the future. As she put it, "There were times when life was so black, I didn't know how to hold on, and I lost hope. They hoped for me, and believed for me. They really believed that, as long as my heart wanted God, He would bless me, and it didn't matter how I felt, or what I had done in the past."

Their belief did carry her through many valleys, but there came a time when she needed to start believing for herself, and feeling God's love. When that time came, she declared, "This may sound strange to you, and I don't begin to understand it myself, but I believe with all my heart that their commitment to believe for me, and their act of doing it, really set my feet on the path to healing and blessing from God."

"No, Rachel" I smiled, "it doesn't sound strange to me at all." And looking out the colonial window into the church yard, I wondered how many times had someone believed for me, when I couldn't believe for myself. My mother had, long before I accepted my call to the ministry. And Carol had, many times. And Cay and Judy at the Community of Jesus had, when I despaired about a seemingly impossible situation in the church. Was that not what the horizontal element of the Christian life was all about? Was that not what those four friends did for the paralytic, when they tore open the roof and lowered him in front of Jesus?

Rachel continued her sharing. "That reminds me of my little brother. When he was a baby and couldn't walk, I would carry him, wherever he needed to go. I loved him and wouldn't let him miss out, just because he didn't have the know-how or strength to walk himself. Those women did the same for me, carrying me to Jesus, until I got to the place where I could begin to believe for myself. It took me awhile to accept that they really cared that much for me. But when I did, I realized that it was God loving me, through them. And then I could believe."

Fortified by the assurance of her 3D group's steadfast love, Rachel was now ready to take the next step, a painful one. Rachel began to get honest with herself, about who she was, without Him. It was not a pretty picture, and always in the past, she had run from the reality of it. But now she had the courage to face it, knowing that the friends God had given her, would not throw stones at her, but would help her to the foot of the Cross, where all were equal and all could change.

There was something perverse about the wind currents over Lake Ontario that encouraged almost any winter storm to dump the maximum load of snow on Rochester. Visitors were appalled, but for the locals, frost-plug heaters in cars and mountains of plowed snow by the roadsides were a winter way of life. This February was no different, I thought, as I walked past snow piles taller than I was, in the church parking lot. Stamping the snow off my boots in the hall, I was just taking off my overcoat, when Diane hurried around the corner.

"Rachel is having contractions, and they've just taken her to the hospital!"

"Reschedule my appointments," I said, pulling my coat back on, "I'm going over there."

I had a tendency to drive quickly anyway, especially when I could excuse it by "being about my Father's business", but that morning I made it to the hospital in under 15 minutes, despite the icy conditions. As I strode into the waiting room, outside the labor room, I saw Grace and Helen there, from Rachel's group. "How's she doing?" I asked, pulling off my coat.

"She's fine; they've just taken her into the delivery room," they calmly reassured me, and I remembered that they'd had many children and several grandchildren.

Soon a nurse emerged, and with a big smile announced: "It's a boy! You can go in and see Rachel in a few moments." We all rejoiced, and standing there in that little waiting room, we joined hands and thanked God for this new gift of life.

When we went in to see Rachel, she was still groggy from the anesthetic, and had an intravenous tube in her arm. But as I approached the bed, she smiled weakly and held my hand tightly. I prayed a simple prayer of gratitude and saw two teardrops of joy come out of the corners of her eyes. Pulling me down so that my ear was near her mouth, she whispered, "I'm going to call him Joshua."

"What a great name!" I exclaimed. "Joshua was a real man of God, full of courage and obedience. How did you pick it? Is he one of your favorite Bible characters?"

She shook her head. "I don't know who he is," she managed, "but I like the name. I want my son to be a follower of the Lord."

When Rachel left the hospital, the women in her group gave her baby clothes and nursery furniture that they had collected, and plenty of boxes of disposable diapers. Joshua would have a good start in life. Best of all, he and his mother were soon invited to move in with a family from the church. I heartily agreed with the invitation. Bud and Bea were a generous, giving couple, with two children of their own, who had opened their home before to foster children and inner city youths. Rachel gathered her things together and took Joshua into the beautiful split-level house which would be their home for the next three years. Joshua shared a room with Eric, their six-year-old, and Rachel had a bedroom to herself with the most beautiful bedspread she had ever seen.

Now began a new step in her life, learning how to live with another Christian family and share the ordinary ups and downs of life. She had never lived with a "normal" family before, and she was looking forward to it. For the first time there seemed to be order and peace in the place where she lived. Oh, Bud and Bea had spats once in a while, but those arguments got resolved, and there was an obvious and successful attempt to live under Christ's direction. Rachel observed how they listened to each other, and tried to prefer the other. Watching them, she also learned to pray about even the smallest matters. In sum, she had become a part of a family that cared about each member, and what she was learning would stand her in good stead one day, when she had a family of her own.

Rachel soon joined the optional Session II of her 3D group. One day, she admitted to the group that she was still frequently harassed by thoughts of men. One of the women told her the same thing that the first group had told her: that since she had no father that she knew, she was looking to men for her security, when she found no security in her home. But she had security in her home-life now, and she had Jesus, Who was all the security she needed. Somehow, this time it made sense, and she asked the group for help in changing her thoughts. They suggested to her that for a period of time, she might try disciplining herself not to see any men.

She told them that she wanted to think about that, before committing herself to take on such a discipline. "Dr. Bill," she said at one of our regular appointments, "it feels right, and I think God wants me to do it. But I'm not sure I can; I think I'll die, because men have always been a part of my life. But," she sighed, "I guess I'm willing. Only pray for me, will you?"

"I will," I assured her. "Have you learned the verse in your group yet about discipline?"

"You mean the one from Hebrews?"

"That's the one: 'All discipline for the moment seems painful, but afterwards it yields the peaceful fruit of righteousness, for those who are trained by it.' Rachel," I said, looking at her, "it *will* be hard for awhile, but if you're faithful in that discipline, God will do a lasting work in you. You know, it's like being addicted to cigarettes or drugs; to break the hold of such things, you have to be free of them for awhile. But once you are, you're going to find that your acceptance and approval comes from God — not men, or women. You'll see that God accepts you, just as you are." Her face lit up at that; finding such acceptance, and approving of herself, were distant dreams which might now come true.

Several weeks passed, before Rachel came to see me again. She was still beaming. When I asked her how things were going, she replied, "It's been hard, Dr. Bill. My life has changed drastically. But I have a regular routine now, and I take care of myself more than I ever did before. The hardest thing has been staying away from men. But I've been able to do it, and I know that because of it, I'm going to have a better life." She paused and then added emphatically, "One thing for sure: Joshua is going to have a much better start than I did!"

"How do you feel about your relationship with God?" I asked her.

She thought for a moment, before replying. "I'm beginning to have an overwhelming sense of His acceptance of me. My past doesn't seem to matter to Him. And every time I go to my group, I have a genuine sense of God's love for me."

Over the months, I watched the gentle fruit of God's love ripen in Rachel's life. She joined the church, and brought Joshua for baptism. Then she enrolled in a course to be a practical nurse. Her natural ability in studies put her in the top part of her class, while at the same time she cared for her young son with the help of the church women.

It was a sunny, warm day in June, when I entered the auditorium at the nursing school. It was an old hall, in need of fresh paint, but when Rachel and the 26 other girls filed in, wearing their white starched uniforms and white nursing caps proudly resting on their heads, the room lit up. One by one, the names were called, and when Rachel rose and went to receive her diploma, I couldn't help standing to my feet and snapping several pictures, just as if I were her father.

Several years later, I had the privilege of standing at the end of the long aisle in the church, and watching Rachel slowly approach on the arm of one of the elders of the church. Beside me, waited a smiling, nervous giant of a man who loved Rachel with his whole heart, and who in a moment would become her husband. Dan was a Christian who had met Rachel at the hospital where she worked. As their friendship developed, they had come to me for counsel. Over the months, Rachel was able to tell him of her background, and he was graced to love and accept her in the midst of it all.

I felt a little choked up, as I recalled the last time I had seen them, only a few days ago. We had had an early snow, and I was in my office, looking out the window at the snow-covered parking lot. A car pulled in, and a big blond man got out. He went around the car, to open the door for his shorter, dark-haired wife, who carried a little baby in her arms. Tenderly, he put his arm around her, to guide her feet on the snow. Joshua had a younger brother now, and thinking back to that first morning, when Rachel had come to my office, I realized that her journey home was complete.

4

KIRSTEN

Sometimes God permits affliction to befall us, not to chastise us, but to prune us for greater service. . . .

All day long, Kirsten had been hard at work around her house, and now she collapsed in her favorite chair in the living room, to rest a bit, before starting supper. She loved the view out the big picture window; from where she sat, she could see the big Mississippi River, running by the edge of their property. And on this warm March afternoon, the normally muddy river took on a a golden hue, as it reflected the last rays of the setting sun.

Kirsten loved her home, situated in a beautiful suburb outside of Minneapolis. After moving five times in 12 years, because of her husband's business, they had finally settled down. Their house was almost perfect. She loved the brick half-front rambler, the spacious foyer, the three bedrooms and fireplace on the first floor, and the two guest and family rooms on the lower level. Best of all, there were open fields behind the house, and in the distance, the headwaters of the mighty Miss.

Kirsten and her husband Hans were Scandinavian, and their house reflected their background. The living room was decorated in soft off-white walls, light blue draperies, trim, and carpet, and two comfortable occasional chairs with blue-and-white upholstery. Looking around the room now, while she rested, Kirsten could not help reflecting on how good life had been to them. Here she was, the wife of a successful owner of a large truck dealership, who was also the part-time mayor of their thriving suburb. She and Hans had raised and educated three children, who were now off on their own. The coming years would be filled with travel, comfort and all those activities which she had not had time to do, while raising the children. God had been good to them, she thought: no big crisis had ever entered their lives — until Hans' business had failed. But even that, as traumatic as it had been, had not ruined them.

Kirsten had known that Hans was having trouble with his business. He had been granted a franchise by the National Truck Company to sell heavy trucks and tractor-trailers five years before. Business had been good; National made quality vehicles. But Hans' contract with them stipulated that he pay a monthly interest of 1% over prime on all his inventory. At first there was no problem, but beginning in 1979, interest rates had soared to 19 and 20%, and he could not sell enough trucks to pay the huge monthly interest payments, called for in the contract.

The squeeze got worse; because of such high interest rates nationally, few truckers and farmers could afford to buy any new equipment. Sales which had always been strong, slowly dried up. All the financial analysts predicted that the Federal Reserve would soon loosen the restrictions on the money supply, and in a few months the rates would fall, and business would boom again. All Hans had to do was hang on and ride out the slump.

He tried; he did everything he could. Borrowing $40,000 from his father to help his cash flow, he hustled truck sales as much as he could. But it wasn't enough. He made the January, February, and March payments, but to do it took everything he could scrape together. And then came April, and there was nothing left. And so, on the first Monday in May, National sent a team to repossess all the vehicles and thousands of dollars worth of spare parts in the dealership, even though Hans had already paid for the parts. That was part of the agreement he had had to sign, to obtain the National franchise. Then the company revoked his franchise license, leaving him nothing to sell except used vehicles and parts.

For six months, he tried to make a go of it, providing first-rate service and selling what he could. But Hans now owned a business that had nothing to sell, and no money to replenish inventory. Though he was by nature optimistic, he had lost his ability to do business, and had no choice but to declare bankruptcy in November. The final ignominy came three months later, when, to satisfy his creditors, he was forced to hold an auction and sell every piece of equipment and every asset of the business.

They had retained their house, and Hans was still an exceptional heavy equipment salesman. Her daydreaming was interrupted by the afternoon's mail falling in through the slot in the front door. She went over and gathered it up, returning to her chair and her view of the river. Flipping through the mail, she tossed aside the junk items which would soon go in the waste basket. Just then, she came to a thick business envelope addressed to Hans, with the name Barton, Barton & Dorfman in the upper left-hand corner. It was obviously a legal firm; why would they be sending something to her husband? As tempted as she was to open it, she left it on the coffee table, for Hans to open when he came home.

She fixed a lovely dinner for the two of them, timed so that it would be ready five minutes after Hans opened the garage door. And on schedule, a few minutes before six, he came in, giving her a kiss and asking if any mail had come. With her wooden stirring spoon, she gestured towards the coffee table in the living room and started to serve their dinner. She was just taking the plates to the table, when she noticed him opening the thick envelope — and watched, as the color drained from his face.

Setting the plates down, she went over to him and asked him what the letter was about. Without saying a word, he handed her the correspondence. Neatly typed on expensive bond stationery with the name of the firm embossed at the top, she read the words, "We wish to notify you that the National Truck Company is bringing suit against you for $1.2 million, to insure its claim for its dealership in Alton."

She dropped the letter and looked at Hans. "This has got to be a mistake! Some computer error — they probably meant $120,000. But we don't even have $12,000 — what's it all about?" Her words trailed off into silence, as she looked at her husband's ashen face.

"It's no mistake," he murmured at last. "A clause in the contract that I had to sign to get the dealership franchise, guaranteed that you and I would be held personally responsible for the full payment on all equipment purchased on time from the dealership. A lot of that debt is still outstanding, and now some of the farmers must have gone into default, just as we did."

Kirsten was furious. "Why didn't you tell me this could happen?" she shouted. "Why did you keep this possibility from me?" She paced back and forth, her voice rising. She knew from experience that if she screamed, he would just leave the room. But she felt hurt and angry, and more than a bit self-righteous. How could he be so stupid, as to let this happen to them? When he protested that she *did* know it could happen, and he had not reminded her of this, because he was just trying to protect her from having to worry, she became more furious. But deep inside, she knew that she wanted to be protected, and not have to think about anything bad. So she had not pressed Hans to find out what was the worst that might happen. Her anger was out of control now, and instead of him leaving the room, she did, slamming the door behind her.

Then she found herself getting angry at the National Truck Company. For fifteen years, it had been like a parent to Hans and Kirsten. From the early days of their marriage, Hans had worked hard for them; in fact, they used to refer to the company as "uncle". She and Hans had put up with moving every three years all around the country. They had disrupted the lives of their children, Hans had given a lot of himself to the company — and after all that, this was what they got in return. It did no good to realize that the relentlessly high interest rates were driving National itself into bankruptcy. In all likelihood, its directors, in a last-ditch effort to stave off corporate disaster, instructed their attorneys to bring suit to recover every last dollar they could. But she could work up little sympathy for National's directors; no matter what happened, they would undoubtedly keep their homes.

Then Kirsten turned her anger on herself. How stupid she had been, to sign a simple piece of paper which agreed that they were both personally responsible for all indebtedness of the dealership's customers. It was the only way Hans could get a franchise, but he and his lawyer had assured her that it was only a technicality; it would never mean anything. Only now it did; there was a $1.2 million suit against them. They could lose their home and the securities they had carefully built up for their retirement years.

Finally, she turned her rage on God. Wasn't He supposed to provide good things for His children? Wasn't He supposed to protect them from things like this? Where was God, when she needed Him? And what of her house? She knew that Christians were not supposed to hold onto material possessions, and she had given up so much, moving as often as they had. But now she had lived in this house for five years — the longest time they had lived anywhere — and she had grown to love it.

Her anger spent, she came back to the living room, went to Hans, and put a hand on his arm. Then she looked around the room again, and realizing that it would soon be sold out from under them, she began to cry. Hans tried to reassure her, but he was as crushed as she was, and could not find any words to help. Their dinner was cold, but they didn't care; silently, they ate a little of it, and cleared the dishes.

During the next few days, Kirsten went through the house, room by room, imagining what special possessions she would want to save, in the likely event that the court ordered an auction of all their belongings. She packed up a set of Danish china which had been in her family a long time and sent it to Hans' parents. After what they had lost in his business, it was the least she she could do for them. Next, she gathered up some beautiful crystal pieces she owned, their fine china, and some items of sterling silver which they had bought at the birth of each child, and carefully wrapping them, she sent them to the children. That done, she felt prepared for the worst.

But it was Hans who was having the harder time with his feelings. Until now, his whole career had been moving steadily upward. He didn't know how to handle a setback of this magnitude, and Kirsten didn't know how to help him. Neither of them mentioned the lawsuit to anyone. Hans was the mayor and was already planning to run for re-election in the spring. What would people think, if it came out that he was being sued for more than a million dollars? Would they say that, if he couldn't manage his own business, how on earth could he manage the town's? Kirsten liked being the mayor's wife; when she went into a store, people would whisper to each other and say, "That's the mayor's wife." Now, because of the lawsuit, Hans might lose. It made her angry all over again.

She was surprised to find that place and position were so important to her. Her mother and father had come separately to America from Norway. When her father arrived at 18, he had worked on a farm in Illinois, to pay off the cost of his passage. When he met her mother, she was working as a house cook and family helper. They married and moved to Minneapolis, and later her father, who was a gifted carpenter, had built his growing family a two-bedroom home.

In her early years, Kirsten was aware that things were difficult financially. Often there was not enough money for gas, and her mother would give the last orange to her children and go without herself. But Kirsten's father worked hard as a laborer and shipfitter, and finally used every bit of his meager resources to acquire a small cement block plant. With that, things had started to improve.

Kirsten was proud of her parents' accomplishments, and when she met Hans, she wanted them to approve of him. Hans had been president of the Young Republican Club at college, and president of his fraternity. It seemed that everything he did succeeded. It was that way after they got married, too, and she could hardly bring herself to tell them of his franchise going under. But now the lawyers' letter coming on top of that was too much; she just couldn't tell them about it.

During those dark days following the letter, the Holy Spirit reminded Kirsten of her commitment to Christ, and of the Lord's leadership in her life. When she was a little girl, her grandmother had taken her to church. She heard the preacher talk a lot about hell, and so when she was 12, she asked to be baptized, believing that she would thus escape that fiery fate. When she got married, she had some faint sense that God had brought her and Hans together. But both of them liked to have a good time and enjoyed parties, and so they gave little serious thought to God in their daily lives.

The thought came to her: *was* she a Christian? Well, of course she was! Didn't they go to church, wherever they were living? Didn't she join the choir and participate in events at the church? She was an American, wasn't she? She must be a Christian!

But now, thinking back over their life, she wondered if she had really been happy. If she was going to be honest with herself, the answer would have to be no. It had not been many years into their marriage that Kirsten had begun to feel dissatisfied. As she began to listen to the leaders of the emerging feminist movement, she felt cramped and imprisoned in her circumstances. To make matters worse, Hans didn't communicate with her much. Nor did he really pay attention to her or care for her; it seemed his business was his life.

Growing increasingly discontent, she had read some of the new trendy literature which espoused divorce as being good for a couple. Continuing along that train of thought, she had began to imagine what she would do, if she were free, and that led to fantasizing about old boyfriends — especially one whom she had gone with for a long time. She had imagined how exciting life would be with him, living in luxury and having everything she wanted. Since Hans had been scheduled to be transferred to Washington D.C. soon, where her former boyfriend lived, she fantasized meeting him — secretly, and beginning a romance again. By that time, she wanted out of her marriage, and that would be a way to do it.

But God's plan for Kirsten did not exactly coincide with the then-current feminist thinking, and while she did not yet know Him personally, He was no less in charge of the circumstances in her life. Shortly after moving to Washington, Hans and Kirsten joined a nearby Episcopal Church. A woman invited her to attend a prayer group, and there she met several women her age who seemed to know Christ well enough to talk to Him in prayer. Kirsten found herself hungering for such a relationship. One Wednesday, at the end of their prayer session, she bowed her head and quietly asked Christ to take charge of her life. She yielded to Him all her desires, fantasies, and dreams, and gave over her life to His control.

After her commitment, Kirsten was faced with doing the hardest thing she had ever done: becoming obedient to the Lord. Always before, she had managed to get her own way; now, she had to listen to God. And one of the first things she knew she had to do, was put away her fantasies of another man. Fantasy had always been her way of escaping the unpleasant reality of the moment, and she had excused it as being far less harmful than the addictive escapes others used — alcohol, drugs, sleep, or even busyness.

But now the new Master of her life was calling her to live in reality; to do otherwise, was to open herself to the enemy of her soul. Reality was often painful, but she would not be walking through it alone. He would be there, by her side, and He would guide her by His Spirit and comfort her with His grace. To Kirsten, it was a whole new way of looking at life. But she could see it working in the lives of her friends in the prayer group, and it was a way that she wanted sufficiently to give up her fantasy.

The second change which the Lord now seemed to require of her concerned Hans. Looking at their marriage in reality, Kirsten had to admit that she didn't really like her husband, and seldom listened to him or honored his requests. Now she was convicted that she had to start caring for him. It turned out to be more difficult than she had imagined, for she had spent so much of her life caring only for herself. Also Hans seemed remarkably self-sufficient, and appeared quite content to care for himself. But she persevered — for she realized that her dissatisfaction with her marriage was primarily due to her lack of care for Hans, and her total self-centeredness.

Like all of us, Kirsten expected change to occur quickly. It didn't, especially not in Hans. But as the weeks went by, and she kept at it, she did begin to feel a distinct change taking place in her own heart. And that change manifested itself in discernible symptoms. Instead of sleeping in each morning, she got up and made breakfast for Hans. That symptom, he noticed, as in the past he practically had to drag her out of bed. She also began to ask him about his concerns, and to pray for him, when he was at work. She read her Bible faithfully now, and went to church more often, and began to party less. In fact, when she drank, she got sick; that had never happened before.

Eventually, Hans did acknowledge the change in her — but didn't like it. Her new spiritual emphasis seemed threatening to him, and sometimes it made him angry. One day, about a year after Kirsten's new commitment, he met with their rector, to talk about the problem. It was during that session that he, too, ended up making a commitment of his life to the Lordship of Christ.

So both Hans and Kirsten were more or less committed Christians, when the lawyers' letter arrived. But in the days that followed, as they waited for a court date to be set for a hearing, their faith was not sufficient to keep them from sinking into the depths of despair. To take his mind off things, Hans turned to an entirely new area of selling — real estate, and he seemed to have a gift for it. Maybe things would get better; the few Christian friends in whom they had confided about their crisis, assured them they were praying for them, and that God would come to their rescue and not let them suffer any more pain. But as much as she appreciated their reassurances and wanted to believe them — she couldn't.

For Kirsten had grown up with a strong work ethic implanted in her. People could succeed at anything they chose to, if they were willing to work hard enough for it. If someone failed, it was either because he didn't work hard enough, or it was the result of a moral failure in that life. To Kirsten, there was no other explanation.

Consequently, she assumed that she must have done something grievously wrong, for God to permit this to happen to them, and she spent hours in introspection, hoping that if she found out what her sin was and confessed it, the lawsuit would be withdrawn, and Hans could resume his business. When that didn't work, she focused again on Hans. *He* must have done something terrible and was hiding it from her, and God was trying to uncover it. For several weeks, she speculated on what awful thing he could have done, but got nowhere.

The problem was, Kirsten had no understanding of the role of suffering in the Christian life. For her, to be a Christian was to be assured of a pleasant, trouble-free life. Didn't the Bible say they were members of a royal priesthood? She was a princess and her husband was a prince. They would have all that they wanted, and God would make it happen. And, for a while, it had appeared that He had. But then, suddenly, reality burst this make-believe bubble.

And now she was tormented by her own thinking. *Why*, she kept asking? Why had God allowed this to happen to them? Was He angry at them? Punishing them? If so, for what? What did God want of them? And so it went, as Kirsten joined ancient Job, in asking the same questions he had thousands of years before.

During the darkest night of that period, Kirsten had a dream. She saw the house where she grew up, and saw her mother standing at the large picture window in the living room, looking out to the front yard. Her father was in the yard, pruning the evergreen trees and bushes, which he did every year. In her dream, her mother was pounding on the glass window, saying loudly, "Gus don't! Gus don't!" But he didn't stop, and after he was done with the pruning, the bushes looked awful. But Kirsten figured that he knew what he was doing, and what sort of pruning the bushes needed.

When she awoke, Kirsten was transfixed by the dream. It was so clear and seemingly significant that she sensed it had been sent by God. But what did it mean? What was He trying to show her? Then, in a flash, it came to her! The bushes and trees hadn't done anything wrong. The pruning her father was doing was for their good, and not meant as a punishment. Then she remembered the words of Jesus in John 15: "I am the vine, and my Father is the vinedresser. Every branch of mine that bears no fruit, He takes away, and every branch that does bear fruit, He prunes, that it may bear more fruit."

And then she saw it all: all that was happening to them, and that which well might happen to them soon, was part of God's pruning. He knew how to make them more fruitful. He knew what dead wood in their lives needed to be cut off, what producing vines needed to be pruned, to bring more fruit. He knew what was best for Hans and Kirsten, and through all that was happening to them, He loved them. She almost exploded inside with the promise that God gave her that morning!

A month later, Kirsten found herself at a national 3D conference for group leaders in Rochester. In her small, evangelical church in Alton, at the request of her pastor, she had become a co-leader of a 3D group. After a year of leading groups, and feeling the need to refresh her skills, she eagerly signed up with her co-leader, Priscilla, to attend the leaders' conference. Although she had been to many business conferences with Hans, she had never been to one on her own, and she was excited — and relieved to get away from the constant pressure of the impending lawsuit.

I met Kirsten at the conference after the opening speech. As it happened, her pastor's parents were members of Parkminster Church, and they brought her over to meet Carol and me. She had blond hair and a Nordic face, and while appearing calm outwardly, there were tension marks around her eyes which told me she was load of worry. After exchanging greetings. I expressed the hope that the weekend would help her obtain some answers. She thought I meant answers about 3D, but I meant solutions to her inward dilemma.

On the first night, the conferees saw a video of a talk show on sibling jealousy. Here she had come to the conference to learn more about leading a group, and she was pierced in her heart by the truth about her jealousy of her brother. All her life she had tried to hide it from herself, but she could see it so clearly in the tape, that she had to admit that her younger brother had been the favorite of the family — and still was. Her parents had always wanted a boy. And come to think of it, her grandmother also obviously loved him more than her. She even recalled her mother telling her that when she was born, she was not named for two months because her parents had been so sure she would be a boy.

Kirsten was shocked, but relieved to have all this come to the surface, after having been buried for so long. That night she confessed her jealousy and rivalry to God — and for the first time felt free, when she thought of her brother. That revelation alone would have been worth the trip to Rochester, but it would not be the only surprise for Kirsten.

The next day, the conference leaders announced that counseling was available that afternoon, for anyone who wanted it. Kirsten signed up, hoping against hope that whoever she talked to, would have a word of prophecy for her, to encourage her in the midst of her despair about the lawsuit. When the time came for her counseling appointment, she was ushered into a small room off the main assembly hall, which was apparently used as a library for Sunday School materials. Shelves on two walls were crammed with books, leaflets, pictures, craft supplies and art work, and a gray four-drawer file cabinet stood guard by the door.

Her counselors introduced themselves as two lay people from the host church, and Kirsten was mildly disappointed, having hoped that one of the church's ministers or the director of 3D, would counsel her. She started talking superficially, hoping that the Holy Spirit would appear with a prophecy or a word of knowledge for her.

Suddenly, in the midst of her empty chatter, Kirsten found herself pouring out her story about the situation back home, expressing all her hurt and fear and anger. She did not really hear most of what they said to her in reply, but she did hear them talking about her self-pity. And now, as the counseling session drew to a close, God began to convict her of how much she felt she was a victim of circumstances. She started mentally recalling how good she had been — going to church, tithing, and doing good works in the community, and that triggered all her feelings of self-pity and "poor me" which had been stored up for the past few months.

For the first time, she was consciously in touch with how much she felt that what had happened was unfair, and how much she felt she didn't deserve it. She saw how much she accused God in her self-pity, and how much she had believed that her behavior should merit better treatment. All at once those attitudes were repugnant to her. She saw how much she had offended God. Bowing her head, and in front of the counselors, she confessed her sins. Immediately she sensed a great burden being lifted, and she felt much lighter inside.

On her return to Alton, Kirsten continued on in her daily routine, still waiting for some resolution of the court case. Nothing had happened in the year and a half since the company had announced that they were suing for $1.2 million, and Hans' lawyer said the case could well drag on for another year, since the court docket was so backlogged.

A year before, Hans had been re-elected mayor, and now the party leaders urged him to run for the state legislature. They liked his enthusiasm and his successful record — and they needed a fresh face to challenge the incumbent in his district. Apparently his business failure was not a problem with the voters.

Just as soon as Kirsten returned from the 3D conference, Hans launched his campaign, and she threw all her energies into assisting her husband, believing it was good therapy to concentrate on something which offered promise, instead of dismal failure. She went door to door, asking people to vote for her husband, and cheerfully endured the grueling work of licking stamps, and mailing campaign literature. She organized groups to meet her husband, and arranged all his speaking engagements.

On election night, she and Hans and the children all gathered in the family room to watch the results. In the beginning, Hans was leading the race, but as the hours went on, his lead slowly dwindled, until at the end he lost by 20,000 votes. Another bitter blow — when would the string of them cease? Not right away, it seemed, for Kirsten was called to the bedside of her dad, who died shortly afterwards.

Several weeks after her father's death, my wife and Lorie, two directors for 3D, came to Alton to lead a workshop and stayed at Kirsten's home. After the meeting one evening, they relaxed in the family room with Kirsten. The three of them were sipping coffee, when Kirsten began to describe the series of setbacks which had happened to her family, just since the conference in Rochester, the year before. The more she talked, the more agitated she became, until Carol broke in to ask her about the object of her obvious anger. Surprised, Kirsten thought for a few moments, and then, in an almost inaudible voice, she admitted, "I'm angry at God." With that, she broke down and cried.

The two women ministered the love and compassion of Jesus to her. She confessed her anger, received God's forgiveness, and again felt relieved of the pressure of her feelings, and of guilt which she had been carrying for a long time. It was hard for her to say goodbye to Carol and Lorie the next day, because of all the help they had brought her.

Two years and one month after Hans and Kirsten first received that fateful legal letter, the lawsuit finally came to court. A young Christian attorney represented them. The judge heard all the arguments from both sides, and finally ruled that the judgment should be reduced to $50,000, payable over the next twenty years. He also admonished the National Truck Company for treating an employee so badly.

With the suit at last settled, Hans could close the book on his failure as a truck dealer, and he thanked God for his new career. Today, as a real estate agent, he is more successful than he has ever been in his life.

Even more important, Kirsten called me recently and said that both of them have accepted the pruning God did in their lives. It has made them deeper, more committed followers of Christ, and more effective ones as well.

The lessons that God taught them through their trials and sufferings has made them trust Christ more than ever before. He has worked compassion into the very fiber of their being, and they can effectively counsel others now, because of the mercy and understanding in their hearts. In a recent letter, Kirsten summed it up: "What a happy, happy thing it is to be able to come into the reality of what being a Christian is! Thank you, Jesus, for the real me I am becoming, because of You."

5

BET

Is there life after death? When a beloved spouse dies, there is — and must be — meaningful life for the survivor. The secret is finding it.

Almost from the beginning of my ministry in Rochester, Bet and Bob had been close friends of ours. We had scarcely moved into our new manse, when Bet came over with a pan full of lasagna for our family. Then Bob dropped by to tell me where I could get my car serviced. During the next several months, Bob would often stop by with helpful suggestions, or volunteer to help me on many projects around the house or church.

Bob was that way. A printer by trade, he was naturally handy in many areas, and he loved the church. Besides being the tenor soloist in the choir, he served as an elder and the Sunday School superintendent. Full of life, with plenty of energy, Bob was creative and loved to do things with his hands, as well as sing his heart out.

His wife Bet was more reserved, but helped out in Sunday School, while raising five children. She was a good mother and homemaker, though sometimes she seemed a bit frazzled. She leaned on Bob for help in disciplining their four boys and in maintaining the house, and relied on him to keep track of the family finances and make the major decisions about cars and appliances.

Since our children were about the same age as theirs, we often went on picnics together, and once even ventured to vacation together on Cape Cod. Bob and Bet were also in a small prayer group with us, and after we had begun to trust each other, we exposed our problems and our faults to each other, seeking God's answers. Just as it is often easier to see the problems in other people's children than in our own, we were learning that we could help each other see ourselves as others see us. Many times God would speak through one of us, to provide wisdom or truth for the other. Of course, that depended on us trusting each other, and *listening* to each other, as carefully as if God Himself were speaking to us — as indeed He often was. One dark, rainy Monday in November, three days before Thanksgiving, I felt an urgent need to go and see Bet and Bob. The previous evening, Bob had carried Bet into our small group meeting, because she had twisted her ankle and couldn't walk. Now, sitting at my desk, I felt compelled to go and pray for her. I asked Carol to come with me, and together we knocked on the door of their modest home. Bob worked the second shift from 3 to 11 p.m., and it was he who came to the door. A little surprised to see us, he nonetheless warmly welcomed us and took us into the living room, where Bet was propped up in a recliner, her ankle red and swollen. We chatted for a bit, and then I asked if I could pray for her ankle. She agreed, and Bob, Carol, and I laid hands on the puffy skin and asked God to touch it and heal it.

In my former congregation, I had prayed for God's healing for many people, but this time was different; I was a new pastor, and didn't want to offend any of my new parishioners. As far as I knew, nobody in my new congregation knew about divine healing, but the urging I felt seemed like the Holy Spirit. Would this couple, who were now our friends, understand? I felt it was another risk worth taking, so I explained to them that the Bible said to pray for healing, and I trusted God to put their hearts at peace about it.

It was almost noon, as we said goodbye, and Bob thanked us and told us that he had made an appointment to take Bet in to see the doctor, later that afternoon, and he would let us know what he said. As Carol and I drove home, we talked rather hesitantly about what we had done. Would word spread to the congregation that the new minister was some strange person who was a "faith healer"? Would this turn off our new friends? Would God heal her?

We knew that God did heal, and that He had answered our prayers for physical healing in the past. But each time was a totally new situation, with many aspects and ramifications that only He could know. Sometimes, it was not in His plan or His timing to do a physical healing; sometimes a far greater spiritual healing could be accomplished, if the prayer for physical healing was *not* answered. Sometimes the physical disability was only an external manifestation of a deep need for inner healing. . . . The more we prayed for healing, the more aware we became of the unfathomable depths of His working. He *would* heal, but as Cowper wrote, "God moves in a mysterious way, His wonders to perform."

Late that afternoon, just as I was getting ready to go home, Bob called excitedly, to tell me that the swelling in Bet's ankle had gone down dramatically; in fact, she was walking around on it without pain, and he had cancelled the doctor's appointment. "Praise God!" I shouted and called Carol to tell her the good news. I was especially pleased, because this appeared to be an encouragement from God, that praying for the sick and divine healing was to be a significant part of our ministry in the new church.

After Bet's healing, she and Bob were even closer friends, and I thanked God for the support that they were to the ministry of the church. In many ways, they seemed to be the ideal church family, with no great trauma to test or upset the family structure. And then one evening in February, one of the elders called: several of the men in our church, including Bob, had been playing basketball in a nearby school gym, and Bob had fainted and felt very tired and out of breath. Not wanting to alarm his wife, Bob wondered if he might come over and rest a bit at our house, before going home.

Of course, we said, and they brought him over. When they arrived, we laid Bob, looking pale and faint, on our living room sofa, and gathered around him to pray for an improvement in his condition. Within a half hour, his color had returned, and he was able to sit up. He felt good enough to go home, and we let him, all of us urging him to see his doctor as soon as possible.

Bob did not tell Bet about his fainting spell at first, nor did he contact his doctor, for he had convinced himself that his only problem was too much work, too hectic a schedule, and too much weight around his middle. But the elders and I kept after him to see a doctor, until finally, with great reluctance, he made an appointment. Unable to give Bob any definite answers, the doctor was sufficiently concerned to schedule him for a series of hospital tests and further consultation with heart and lung specialists. All the while, Bob stayed home from work on sick leave and complained of fatigue and shortness of breath. Life was forced into slow motion for this 44-year-old, who had once been so full of energy and vitality; now the simplest aspects of daily living required a supreme effort.

A month later, the heaviest blow came. Bet was at our house that drizzly March day. The phone rang, I answered it and gave it to her. "This is Dr. Morse," her caller introduced himself. "We've completed our studies of your husband's test results, and I'm afraid he is in very serious condition." He paused and then said, "I'm sorry to have to tell you this, but I would suggest that your husband get his affairs in order."

"What do you mean?" Bet gasped.

"I mean, be sure his insurance is up to date, and any other business that's not finished, should be concluded quickly."

Bet collapsed in a chair, and I had to take the phone from her. I identified myself as her pastor, and he repeated the explanation to me, after which I thanked him and hung up, for Bet was in shock. When she could talk, she told us that she had thought that maybe Bob's trouble was some heart condition, but certainly something that could be fixed with modern medicine.

Bob came in just then, from doing something outside, and as he sat on the same sofa, on which we had laid him that first night a month ago, Bet told him what the doctor had said. Bob, too, was stunned; his eyes began to fill up, and he sat quietly for some time. Finally he spoke, and the tone of his voice betrayed a mixture of anger and fear. "Why me? What have I done to deserve this? And what *is* wrong with me anyhow?" He carried on for some time, venting all the pent-up feelings he had stuffed down inside and kept there, despite our appeals, ever since that first night. Finally, the four of us gathered in a circle, holding hands and committing Bob and Bet to God's care and keeping.

Two more weeks of tests followed. Just before one of them, I visited Bob in the hospital and found him in fairly good spirits, having had many visitors from the church and being surrounded by cards and flowers. I noted that he had his devotional books stacked by the side of the bed, and I chuckled, "Bob, if you read all those books, you'll be so holy, you'll float away on a cloud, and they'll never find out what's wrong with you!"

He laughed, and just then the doctor entered the room. "Bob, " he said, "I'm glad your pastor is here, because I'm going to give it to you straight: we've finally diagnosed your case, and you have hypertension of the lungs. What's more, it's a deteriorating situation, and it's fatal; no cure has been found, although there are some experimental drugs which may have some promise."

When the full weight of the words sank in, Bob asked, "What does hypertension mean, doctor?"

"It means that your blood is not getting enough oxygen from your lungs. That's why you've been feeling so exhausted. All we can do now is try to help your lungs to function better." After a little more conversation, the doctor outlined a program of experimental medication and told Bob that he could go home in the morning.

Bob stared out of the window. His working days were over; the question now was how much time he had left. He stared out the window, and nothing I could say at that moment could help him, so I prayed for him. Just then, the phone rang; it was Father Lane, chaplain of the Community of Jesus, on Cape Cod. Bob and Bet had often gone to the Community for retreats and spiritual help. The members there maintained a 24-hour prayer vigil, and when Bob's physical difficulties had begun, Bet had called and asked that he be put on it. Now Father Lane called, and after hearing his prognosis, said that the directors of the Community wanted to offer Bob and his family a place to stay, while he was being treated for his sickness. Boston had some of the best medical treatment available in the nation, and the atmosphere at the Community would be spiritually healing for Bob, as well.

Bob relayed this information to me, and I nodded my approval, knowing that he had had good experiences on his retreats there, and had spoken of sensing the presence of Jesus there. He thanked Father Lane and agreed that it made sense, and that he was sure that Bet would agree, too. When he hung up, for the first time I saw some hope in his face.

It was not easy for the family to uproot after living 20 years in the same place. Their two eldest sons, having completed school and started their careers, would remain behind. While the packing was going on and other preparations were being made, Bob and his family moved in with us at the manse. Church members joined in and provided all kinds of help. Finally, the April day arrived when the U-Haul truck was loaded and ready, with one of Bob's sons at the wheel. Bet climbed behind the wheel of their crammed station wagon, and off the caravan went, to make a new home and to face an uncertain future on Cape Cod.

It didn't take long to settle in at the Community. The members were very caring, and the children were quickly enrolled in school. Household furnishings were put in place, and outwardly life resumed in a reasonably normal fashion. Bob was learning patience, for everything now had to be done in slow motion. Though it was strenuous and taxed his lungs, he sang with the choir, pleading that it was the thing he enjoyed more than anything in the world. So he attended every practice and was in his place in the choir stalls every Sunday. He could not be actively involved in the Community's printing fellowship, as he would have liked, but he could stuff envelopes, and he often helped with mass mailings the Community sent out. Indeed, as long as he could work at his own pace, there were many tasks that he could do. And work he did; in fact, so much was his self-worth tied up in what he could contribute that he was almost obsessive about it.

Each week, Bet would drive him up to Boston, where he would meet with specialists, and it seemed that almost every month there was a new medicine to try. After each trip, both Bob and Bet would find a glimmer of hope sprouting in their hearts.

But the truth was that Bob was slowly losing his grip on life. Almost visibly, the energy which had once been so abundant in him, was draining out, a day at a time. He continued the struggle, but it was a losing battle, and in his heart, he knew it.

The beginning of a new year arrived, and Bob joined the choir in singing for the service on New Year's Eve. But the next day, he came down with a cold and was so miserable, he couldn't eat. The Community doctor hospitalized him the next day, and Bet told me later, about the events of the next several days.

It was a terrible day when she went with the doctor and Bob to the hospital; the snow was blowing, and the air was full of bone-chilling moisture. They had been through this routine for tests so many times in the past several months that she was almost an expert on hospital admissions, but somehow today was different. She stayed with Bob all afternoon in his room. He was feeling poorly, stuffed up with some kind of congestion, and it was with reluctance that she said goodbye to him, and went home.

When she returned in the morning, she was heartened to hear from the nurse that he had had a good night. She fed him his lunch, but he wasn't hungry, complaining of heartburn. "Then," Bet told me, "I saw him struggling for breath. I called the nurse, and she came quickly, and suggested I leave the room. I leaned over Bob's bed and kissed him, and asked God to help him."

She stopped, seeing the scene again in her mind's eye. "There was a flurry of activity in and out of Bob's room," she went on, "and finally the doctor came out, slowly shaking his head. 'I'm sorry,' he said, 'we did all we could, but we couldn't save him.' " Bet started to sob — the deep, convulsive crying that had been repressed in her ever since that day in Rochester, when she first heard the prognosis. The thing she feared the most had come upon her; her husband and beloved companion of 27 years was gone. She knew he was with the Lord. She knew even now that he was singing the songs of Zion. But she was left alone, for the rest of her life. All that they had planned and hoped for together, would never be.

In a daze, she sat in that small waiting room with the dirty ashtrays and burn marks in the rug. That was the rest of her life, she thought. Outside the window, the sun was shining, but it was shining for others, for whom life was going on and still held promise.

Someone had called Father Lane, and now he appeared, when she needed him most. He had suffered similar losses in his own life, and well knew what she was feeling. He put an arm around her, and she buried her face in his shoulder and cried and cried. There was grace on her, during the funeral time and for several days afterwards. Other than a lump in her throat and an ache in her chest, she felt all right and was able to manage each day reasonably well. "And then one day, it hit me," she recalled. "I was filling out a form, and in the blank describing my marital status, I had to put widow. How I hated that word! Here I was, a widow with five children. And I'm only 47! I didn't want to be a widow. I just wanted Bob. I wanted to finish my life, as I had planned. After all, we had raised most of the children and gone through the hard times; wasn't it time now to enjoy the benefits of all those hard years?" As Bet talked, I could see the tension that still gripped her. "I'd go to bed at night," she continued, "and he was not there beside me. There was an empty place at the dinner table. Something would come up, concerning the children, and I'd want to talk it over with him. And he wasn't there."

How I wished that there was something I could say which would ease her suffering! I could tell her to pour her heart out to Jesus — but she was already doing that. The sad thing about deep grief was that there was no shortcut through it, no magic-wand formula to make it quickly over. Pain accompanied life coming into the world, and pain accompanied its leaving, and there was no way to curtail the latter. The important thing was to recognize the grief and express it and be patient — there was a season for grieving, and then that season would end. I was glad that Bet had entered the season, and I prayed that God was give her abundant grace, as she went through it.

She told me that there were days, when she simply did not know how to cope with the daily routine, and I was grateful that she was surrounded by a community of caring people, who could help her. But I also knew that she still had a lot to go through, before she could come to a place of healing. It struck me then, that Bob had already received his healing. He was in the presence of God where, the Psalmist says, "there is fullness of joy." In the meantime, Bet's heart was broken and her life shattered. She was angry with God and all the world for what had happened to her.

Several months passed before I visited the Cape again. She had been through much emotion and was not over the difficult period yet, but I could see now, that she was on her way. Her face was not as tense, her manner was more relaxed, and some of the anger had gone out of her eyes. "What's been going on in you," I asked, "since I saw you last?"

"It's been difficult," she admitted. "I spent many days asking why — and I found myself over and over again, getting angry at God. That surprised me. I had always been a good Christian and never knew I could direct my anger to God. But I kept saying, hadn't we tried to do right? Didn't we both work hard in the church? Why was I being punished this way? Why didn't God allow the husbands of bad people to die, instead of mine? It just wasn't fair."

The more she asked those unanswerable questions, the angrier she got at God. Fortunately, the people in whose house she lived, really cared for her and did not condemn her for speaking that way. They had mercy, for they, too, had been that angry at God, at times. Gently, after each outburst, they would gently lead her in prayer, and she would ask God to forgive her. "I knew Jesus had died for me," declared. "I knew this life wasn't the end. But it still hurt so much to be without Bob, that I felt like shaking my fist at Him, for taking him from me. My outbursts were ugly, but I felt better, releasing all that was pent up within me. And I felt God's forgiveness. And my friends stuck with me."

As she talked, I could hear the relief in Bet's voice. In the years I had known her, she had never been one for expressing feelings outwardly. As a child, she had been the favorite of her father, and had learned how to be a good girl at an early age. Early on, she had learned to keep whatever she felt, inside, and there it remained. She had never wanted to upset her father in any way, but now she was shaking her fist at her heavenly Father — and then asking His forgiveness. It was much more healthy that way, and it was good to see that she was becoming more real.

Bet continued, "After my anger, I went through a period of helplessness. I couldn't do *anything* by myself. Keeping a checkbook was a total mystery to me; Bob had always done that. We needed a new car, but Bob had always taken care of the cars." She smiled. "But you know, every time I needed to do something which I didn't know how to do, I made myself ask for help. And the Lord was good: there was always someone in the Community, who would be able to go with me, or else show me how to do the impossible task. But, oh, was it hard on my pride!"

Slowly Bet began to see that she had spent her life not being needy, looking instead like she was entirely capable. "If I couldn't do something, I would call on Bob and let him do it. I had never really experienced calling on Jesus before, like I had to now. And I did have to; there was no other choice. But you know what?" She looked at me, her eyes shining. "He was — and is — *always* there. And He feels so much closer to me now, than He ever did before Bob's death."

"Bet," I shook my head and smiled, "we've been friends for a long time, and we've shared many happy and sad times together. But I've got to tell you something: you seem more alive to me now, than you ever did before. I wish there were some other way of saying it, but the truth is, Jesus seems so much more a part of your life. I think that, in your life with Bob, before he got sick, you must have put all your faith and trust in him. Well," I added, seeing dismay in her face, "that's not so surprising; we all do it to some degree. But now you've tested God and found Him to be reliable — and very near. And I doubt that it's something you would ever have experienced, were Bob still alive."

Bet thought for a moment, then nodded. "Bill, you know our oldest son recently got a divorce, and our second son lost his job at the same time. When those two things happened, I almost panicked and lost all the healing that I was receiving. I felt that, somehow I had to do something to help them. Had Bob been here, we would have talked and made a plan of action. Instead, I talked out my fear and anxieties to God, and to the people in my house. They helped me see that I didn't have to handle it; God was in charge. I'm slowly learning how to live that way. It's not easy, but I know that it's God's way. And I'm grateful to Him, for the people He has placed around me."

I continued to see Bet and her two youngest children often after that. Gradually, she emerged out of her despair and hopelessness. Almost two years later, I had another conversation with her. It was a sunny afternoon, and we were sitting on her porch overlooking Cape Cod Bay, and having iced tea. She was a typical Cape Codder now, clad in a striped summer dress with colorful sandals, and with the bronzed look of every summer resident. Her hair was speckled with gray now, but she had the same bright eyes and look of peace and healing that she had before.

"You know, Bet, it's been almost three years since Bob died. And I imagine you must still miss him — at times very much. But are there any other places where you're still struggling?"

Bet looked out at the shimmering surface of the bay. "Sometimes I still have trouble in social situations. I always thought of myself as an outgoing person. You remember, I was a cheerleader in high school. And at church, you know how many things I was involved in. But now, sometimes, I feel uncomfortable, entering a room full of people, because I don't know what to do, or where to go." She looked at me, tilting her head. "You know what? I must have hidden behind my husband's friendly personality. I'm coming to see that I'm not the person I thought I was." She took a sip of tea. "Sometimes, when I feel like a fifth wheel around other couples, I get angry all over again about not having a husband. I find myself getting jealous of older couples I see in the supermarket, shopping together. I start to go down with self-pity, realizing that I will never have a husband to grow old with."

Out on the bay, a distant sailboat was running before the wind. "What do you do with those feelings?" I asked, without looking at her.

"When these things happen, the first thing I feel like doing is withdrawing. I want to leave the party, or I want to leave the store. But I've learned that, if I'm ever going to get healed, I've got to stay in those uncomfortable places. So I call on Jesus to help me, and He does, and gives me the grace to stick it out."

What was the worst time of all?

"That's easy: Christmas. Last winter, going Christmas shopping, I found myself longing to buy a special gift for Bob. Everyone around me seemed so happy, and again I would especially notice the couples. It seemed that the whole mall was filled with them! But there were other times, too — when I would come home and find myself snapping at people in the house. I'd sense that I was down, and not know why. Then I would check the calendar and see that it was my birthday, or Bob's, or our anniversary, or even the date of his death. And I would understand why I was feeling that way. Again, I would beg Jesus to help me, and He did. He understood."

"So, where are you now, Bet?" I asked, smiling at her.

She finished her tea, and said, "Frankly, I don't know how I could have gone through losing my husband, without knowing the Lord. He has used this experience to bring me closer to Him, and in that sense, it has been worth it." She got up and stretched. "I still can't say that I don't get depressed or feel sorry for myself. But those times are less now, thank God."

She looked out at the sailboat, as it came about and tacked into the wind. Sensing that there was something else, something more, I waited, to see if she would bring it up.

"I guess the most important thing I've learned" she said, turning back to me, "is to be real with myself and my friends, about how I'm feeling. I don't have to pretend anymore. And because I've been willing to just be me, with all my ugly feelings, I've experienced the reality of God's forgiveness in a way that I never had before. It means something to me now. I've depended on the Lord more in these past three years than in all of my Christian life, and you know, He's never let me down."

I came away from that time with Bet, deeply moved and encouraged at the way God was healing her. None of us, I thought, could guarantee our own existence or that of our family. How would I feel if Carol were to suddenly die? Would I, too, feel lost and alone? So bereft that I would not want to go on living?

Then I remembered what Solomon wrote: God was a "friend that sticks closer than a brother." That was the key. If I depended on Carol or my children or anyone else, I was bound to be disappointed. For death could take away any loved one, on whom I relied. But God could never be taken away by death. Jesus told his disciples that "I will never leave you nor forsake you."

As I walked down the dirt road, leading from Bet's house, I thought about my own priorities, and how much more God needed to be the source of my life.

6
MARK

Trust and obey — sometimes, the latter is much harder....

I was standing in the kitchen of our Cape Cod type manse in Rochester, New York, one Saturday in early September. Carol and I had been called to this suburban congregation just a month before, and it was the fulfillment of a dream. Less than 50 yards from the kitchen window, workmen were erecting a new quarter-million-dollar addition which would become a 500-seat sanctuary, with a large social hall underneath. There was no hiding my excitement at the challenge before me: build up the church, double the attendance, membership and giving, but mainly lead people to Christ, and to a deeper commitment to Him. I would bend every effort, and use all my energy to accomplish the task.

The manse had been built for my predecessor who had founded the congregation and was beloved by all who knew him. Because we had a growing family, the church officials had agreed to make alterations in the house. They turned a first floor bedroom into a dining room, repainted the kitchen, installing new cabinets and a linoleum floor, and finished off the basement, while adding two bedrooms upstairs.

On that September Saturday, I had just finished lunch, and was debating whether to make more calls or prepare my sermon for the following morning, when I was interrupted by a knock on the kitchen door. Carol opened it, and there stood a short, dark-haired man with a moustache, and a vacuum cleaner in his hand. This was my first introduction to Mark.

His manner seemed rather cocky to me. He began, "I'm the Electrolux salesman, and you called for help to repair your machine." I glanced at Carol, who nodded. "So you're the new pastor of this church?" the Electrolux man went on, "Where'd you come from?" I answered that we had recently moved from an inner city church in Bridgeport. "Oh, you wanted to get away from the poor people and the blacks, eh?" he asked flippantly.

Stung, I started to describe all my work in the inner city and my commitment to the poor, but I then realized he wasn't interested. When I asked him about his church commitment, he told me he was a Baptist, adding that he had gone to church all his life. And where did he live? Down the street from our church, about a mile away. As he deftly fixed our vacuum cleaner, he continued to throw off remarks that were sometimes funny and sometimes cutting. I liked his feisty manner, but suspected that his short stature might be contributing to his glib, defiant attitude. As he was leaving I invited him, along with his wife and four children, to attend our church.

Mark and Karen and their children did start coming to our church, and soon joined. We had developed a friendly relationship, and he willingly helped me in any way he could. He had a sharp, quick wit, and I enjoyed the challenge of trading quips with him. Yet at the same time, I sensed he would be willing to be honest with me, and take an honest response in turn.

It was not long before I sensed that Mark was not

doing well in his job selling and servicing vacuum cleaners, and one day he shared with me his frustration at going door to door for sales. After ten years, the market seemed to have dried up. He was making fewer and fewer sales, and things had gotten so bad that when his youngest daughter broke her collarbone, he could not take her to the hospital, because his insurance had lapsed two months before.

Yet God was doing something in this young family. At the depth of their financial crisis, Mark and Karen were convicted by God to tithe what little money they had. They had always pledged to give to the church before, but had never fulfilled it; now, for the first time ever, they paid up their pledge. Soon after that giant step of faith, Mark received a call from Jerry, an elder in the church, asking him to take a job selling tires to garages and gas stations for the largest tire dealer in the city. Believing it was a miracle, and a result of his tithing, Mark gratefully took the job, and for the first time in a long time, began receiving a regular salary.

But, far from his troubles being over, in a way it seemed that they were just beginning. For ten years, Mark had been, in effect, his own boss, and now he had someone else telling him what to do. To make matters worse, he could not stand his new boss, Joe, a hard-driving man who demanded impossible sales quotas. He wanted Mark to call on every customer on his route, twice a month. He wanted Mark to wear a coat and tie. He wanted everything done his way, and he even declared that his way was always right. Worst of all, he did not trust Mark; each day, one of the accounts that he was scheduled to call on, would tell Mark that Joe had called for him, and after a few days Mark realized that Joe was just checking up on him, to see whether he had made his sales calls.

For most of his adult life, Mark had done things his way. He had a total of 20 years of sales experience and firmly believed he knew more about selling than his boss. In selling vacuum cleaners, Mark went where he wanted, when he wanted. He didn't keep a schedule, or maintain a route, and he certainly didn't wear a coat and tie, if he didn't feel it was called for. Best of all, no one checked up on him. He answered only to himself, as to how hard he worked, and anyone who knew him, knew that he worked hard. This new job was driving him crazy, and he frequently thought about his old one, and the freedom that had come with it.

One day, after he had been working for three months, Joe called him into his office at the company's headquarters. It was a spartan office, reeking of stale cigar smoke, with cheap wood paneling and a plain tile floor, and papers and tires and clutter everywhere. Joe motioned Mark to a wall desk in the office and pointed to a telephone on it. "Here," he said, through teeth that clenched a dead cigar, as he handed him a list of a hundred service stations in the area, "I want you to call every one of them now and try to sell them our new #500 tire."

Mark panicked inside, and began to perspire in his face and hands. He hated cold-call selling. He had never been good at it and didn't think it would work. When his boss left, he stared at the phone, read over the list, and decided he needed to go to the bathroom. Then he got a drink of water at the fountain and tried to find a pencil sharpener. He did make one call, but fortunately the line was busy.

An hour later, Joe came back and asked, "Well, how many calls have you made? You should have had five sales by now." Mark got defensive and told Joe that he could make more sales, if he could go in person. His boss got suspicious. "How many calls have you actually made?"

Lowering his head, Mark murmured, "None."

"*What?* I'm going to stay here, until you call everyone on that list, even if it takes all day!" he shouted. And true to his word, he sat across the desk and watched, while Mark dialed each number, using a standard pitch to try and sell the tires.

Mark could hardly stand it. He felt nauseous. His hands gripped the phone so tightly, his knuckles were white. His finger could hardly function to push in the numbers. His voice was choked and almost cracked on several calls. He hated what he was doing and wanted to quit.

Finally, the ordeal was over, and after Mark left his boss's office, he walked down the hall, until he found an empty maintenance room. Slipping into it, for the first time in his adult life, began to weep. Then, remembering Jerry, the man from church who had first invited him to apply for the job, he went over to the warehouse he was in charge of, to see him. Seeing Mark was in trouble, Jerry took him to his office and prayed for God's grace to help him through the difficult time. Mark was surprised to find himself not embarrassed to be in tears in front of a brother in Christ.

Sitting there, he recalled the last time he had really cried. He was ten, and one of his mother's friends had just told him that his father had died. He had started to heave great sobs that seemed to reach to his toes. Then, getting in control of himself, he went over to his mother and said bravely, "Mom, we'll make it." He had felt the burden of care for his mother, since his three older brothers were all in the armed services. That promise had set the tone for much of the rest of Mark's life. He made it through high school by the skin of his teeth. Soon after, he lost his driver's license because of reckless driving and decided to enlist in the Navy at 17. He served in the Philippines and in Saipan, and always underneath was that refrain, "we'll make it." After he was discharged, he started college, but soon majored in ping-pong, becoming champion of the student body, despite the warnings of his student advisor who told him he had to study or flunk out, which he did. He tried again at another local college, this time night school, with the same disastrous results. Now he was feeling failure again, but this time there was a difference: he was with a Christian brother who was asking Christ to help him. He told God — and Jerry — that he would keep trying.

It wasn't long before Mark found himself in another confrontation with his boss. Joe called him in one day and said, "Mark, I want you to sell our #500 tire to Dom's Service Center on Glade Street, and the Acme Discount Auto Center on Main. Sell them a bundle of tires."

Mark winced. He knew the two accounts whom his boss mentioned, and he knew the reputation they had on the street: they were notorious for not paying their bills. He's wrong, Mark thought; they're deadbeats, and after selling for 20 years, he could spot a deadbeat a mile away. "Joe, I think we'd be making a big mistake to extend those two accounts any credit. They've defaulted on a lot of other guys, and they'll do it on us. I know them. Oh, they'll take the tires, all right. But we'll never get paid for them."

Joe clenched his cigar and stared at Mark. "You know the trouble with you?" he asked, and not waiting for an answer, he told him. "You think you know everything. Well, I think you're wrong. Now, why don't you for once stop making excuses and go out there and do what you're being paid for!"

That night Mark could hardly sleep. He told Karen what had happened and reiterated his prediction. By morning, he had decided that he simply could not go through with it, and so he didn't. His turmoil continued throughout the day, but there was no way he was going near those stores.

That evening, Mark was scheduled to meet with one of our church's small Christian sharing groups, of which he and Karen had been a part for six months. He had come to trust the members of the group, and had started to share problems with them, as they did with him. It didn't take long for Mark to blurt out his problem. Describing his boss's foolish demand with great anger, he fully expected everyone in the room to agree with him. Instead, his diatribe was met with a long silence. Then one of the group asked, "Mark, where's Jesus in all of this? What does God want you to do?"

That caught Mark off guard — the thought that the Lord might not agree 100% with him had never entered his head. He knew he was right, and his boss was wrong, and that was the extent of it. "God doesn't want me to do something foolish!" he countered. "He gave me a brain, and He expects me to use it."

Then another member of the group spoke. "Hey, Mark, didn't you tell me you'd just finished reading *Spiritual Authority* by Watchman Nee? And how much it had spoken to you?" Mark nodded. "Well, don't you suppose your boss is one of those 'governing authorities' that Paul says we need to be subject to?" The speaker paused. "You're not going to like this, but I wonder if you're not supposed to do what your boss told you to do, and ask Jesus to change your heart and help you do it."

Mark looked around the group, to see if anyone else felt that way, and it looked like nearly all of them did, although they were waiting for him to ask God inside, and make up his own mind. He didn't want to ask God, because he already sensed what the answer would be; in fact, he had sensed it, the moment he'd been asked where Jesus was. But reluctantly, he did ask God, and still grumbling, he agreed. The group gathered round him and prayed that God would help him do his job.

First thing the next morning, Mark called on Dom's. As he left his car and walked to the office, he had to pray almost constantly, "Jesus, help me." Indeed, he kept repeating it over and over, under his breath. The store manager was delighted to get the new #500 tires, and placed a large order with Mark. And the same thing happened with Acme.

"You see?" crowed Joe, when he returned to the office and reported his sales. "I knew I was right. Mark, all you need is a little confidence, a little gumption! Well, I'm going to see that you get full credit for these sales," and he made a big thing of recording them under Mark's name in the current quarterly sales contest, the prize of which was an all-expense-paid vacation to Bermuda, for the top salesman and his wife.

Two months and countless more inner appeals to Jesus later, Mark was summoned to the company owner's office late one afternoon. He had met Mr. A only once, since starting with the company a year before. "Congratulations, Mark," Mr. A. said, beaming at him from behind the largest desk that Mark had ever seen, "you've won the quarterly sales contest!" Mark could hardly believe it; he had never won anything in his life. "Those sales to Dom's Service Center and Acme Discount pushed you over the top," Mr. A went on, "You're doing a good job; keep it up." Mark left the office, floating on air. He couldn't wait to tell Karen the good news. Bermuda! Who would have believed it? They would go in October, only three months away.

A month later, Joe called him into his office, a sour look on his face. "Mark," he said grimly, "neither Dom's nor Acme have paid for the tires they bought. They were invoiced at net 30, and it's been 90 days now." He drummed his pencil on the desk, as if it were somehow Mark's fault. "I'm afraid we're going to have to repossess whatever inventory they have left."

Everything in Mark wanted to shout "I told you so!" but he squelched the desire, inwardly praying the prayer which had stood him such good stead: Jesus help me!

The next day Mark and Joe took a large company truck with a stake body, and drove up to Dom's and Acme and carted away many of the tires Mark had sold them. It wasn't a pleasant job, and Mark was relieved when it was over.

Only it wasn't over, not quite: two days later, Joe called him in again and told him that he would probably lose his trip to Bermuda, since the repossessed tires would have to be subtracted from his sales figures. Mark was crushed — and furious! On the brink of letting Joe know exactly what he thought of him, he checked himself and fervently prayed his favorite prayer.

Another week passed, and Mark heard nothing. The vacation they had so been looking forward to was now only five weeks away — would they be taking it? Mark would have preferred being told a flat no, than to be kept turning slowly in the wind. Then, on Friday, just before closing time, he was told to report to Mr. A's office. The big boss was in a jovial mood and obviously anxious to leave his office for the weekend. Instead of inviting Mark to have a seat, he simply handed him an envelope, not saying anything, as Mark opened it. In it were two airline tickets to Bermuda.

Mr. A obviously didn't know about the repossessed tires. As much as Mark wanted to take the tickets and run, he said, "Sir, we had to go back and repossess some tires I sold, and I lost the contest, when they were deducted from my sales total. Technically, I don't deserve this."

Mr. A. paused for what seemed like an interminable moment. Finally, he said, "Mark, did you do what your supervisor told you to do?"

"Yes, sir."

"That's all I ask. If the tires came back, that's his problem, not yours. You keep the prize; you've earned it."

In a daze, Mark thanked him and left, silently adding thanks to Jesus, for answering all his prayers.

As Mark related this joyous news to his prayer group, he added that he was beginning to see that all his life he had blamed others for his troubles. In high school, it was the teacher's fault that he didn't receive better grades. In both colleges, the professors were too hard on him, and didn't understand his inability to study. It was the fault of the economy and the shifting market that his sales of vacuum cleaners had dwindled.

Moreover, in his new willingness to see such things, he saw more: in his married life, he blamed Karen for everything that went wrong. In sum, he had spent his entire life, avoiding taking responsibility for his actions and attitudes. But he realized now that he was not a victim of circumstances, and it was *his* attitude that needed changing. And so, he learned what for him was the hardest lesson of all: to point the finger at himself and not at others.

But school had not adjourned. In God's schoolroom, the lessons went on, as long as the student was willing to learn. And as pleased as He was with Mark's progress, He had much more to show him. The company Mark worked for operated 19 retail stores in western New York. The majority of these stores made a profit, but several didn't. Because of his good sales record, Mark was promoted to a store manager the following year, and given a store near his home on a busy main road.

It was not the blessing it at first appeared. This particular store had persistently lost money and had, in fact, run through eight managers in four years. Mark was given three years to bring the store into the black. Grateful for the promotion, he confessed to his group that he was a trifle apprehensive. A salesman to the core, he was sure he would have no problem with that part of it, and that part was obviously the key part to any store. But as for all the administrative details and paperwork, he was not so sure. . . . Scariest of all, of course, was the accountability factor: he would have to accept full responsibility for all that happened in the store. He wouldn't be able to blame anyone else.

Mark knew that managing a store was going to be different from being a salesman, but he did not realize just how different. Oh, he could sell tires; he'd always been able to do that. But now the company expected him to turn in a whole series of regular reports. There was, for instance, the weekly payroll report which was due in the central office every Monday. Then there were monthly reports for sales items outstanding, for inventory control, and reports for monthly budgets for the store. It seemed that every time he turned around, another report was due, and soon overdue, which meant that another administrator in the head office would have to call him and specifically request it.

Mark hated doing the reports, which to him were exactly like homework in school — and he had never done homework, anywhere. He tried to tell himself that it was because he wasn't able to do them, but deep down, he knew the truth: he just didn't *want* to do them. He would go to ridiculous extremes, to avoid doing them, even putting them under a pile of papers on his desk and forgetting them for a few days. Then someone would call, and he would get started on one, only to be interrupted by a customer, or helping one of his employees do a tune-up.

Inevitably Mark's boss was informed of his consistently missing reports. He sent Mark a memo through the interoffice mail: "If you can't deliver this monthly report by next Tuesday, call me." Tuesday came and went, and another memo arrived on Wednesday: "Mark, what happened? You've got to fill out that report. I'll be willing to help you, if you need it. Call me." No response. On Friday, Mark received a call from his boss whose patience had reached its end. He told Mark to get that report in by the end of the day, and not to go home until it was in. Faced with that ultimatim, Mark knuckled down and stayed late into the night, until the report was finished.

That kind of prolonged battle went on for months; in fact, it became almost a perverse game. Mark's boss would start sending pleading notes, then increasingly angry phone calls. As the pressure from his boss increased, Mark would avoid the phone calls he knew were coming. Until finally, he sensed that his boss was so angry, his job was in jeopardy. Then he would do the report. And a couple of weeks later, it would start again.

By this time, Mark had joined a men's 3D group at the church. Every Tuesday evening, ten men would meet for an hour, to weigh in, review their food intake from the week before, listen to a teaching tape, and share their current concerns, ending the meeting on time, with a circle of prayer. Mark had not joined the group because of his weight; that had never been a problem. But he liked the fellowship with other men, and he thought the group might help him live a more consistent Christian life.

It was a cold, snowy March night, when the group gathered in a second floor classroom of the church for their sixth meeting. That night, the leaders decided to ask for sharing first, and Mark did not hesitate, describing the battle he was having, doing his reports. "I'm a good salesman," he told the group, "and I've begun to turn the sales at the store around. In fact, it looks like we're going to be in the black two years ahead of time. But the company wants me to fill out all these ridiculous reports! I'm doing all I can; what more do they want? I can't be bothered to take the time away from selling." On and on he went, building an irrefutable case as to why he was right, and the company was wrong.

As he paused for air, one of the other men cut in and said, "Mark, you're just excusing yourself. Your real problem is that you don't like to be told what to do. You probably never have. You want to do what you want to do, when you want to do it."

The words hit him like a ton of bricks. He wanted to jump up from his seat and pound the speaker, even though the latter was a foot taller. But his anger quickly subsided, because he suddenly remembered his argument with his other boss, about selling those tires to Dom's and Acme, and what God had taught him then about the need to come under authority, and stop accusing and judging everyone else. He told the others about that, and admitted that he had seen back then, that he needed to stop pointing the finger at others and point it at himself, and his own bad attitude. He asked them for prayer.

When it came time for the evening's teaching tape, it started off: "The lesson for tonight is called, 'Nobody Tells Me What To Do!' and is on rebellion. Listen to what the Bible says: 'Rebellion is like the sin of witchcraft. But to obey is better than sacrifice.' "

Mark was dumbstruck; here was coincidence beyond all coincidence! He told God and his friends that he would start proving his repentance, first thing in the morning, and at the end of the meeting, just before the prayer circle, one of the men volunteered to call Mark at work the next day, to see how he was doing.

Mark got to the store even earlier than usual the next morning. He went straight to his desk and started laboriously filling out the first report he could find. As the morning wore on, phone calls came in and customers to distract him, and occasionally he would look up, just to watch the busy flow of traffic. But he kept at it, and when his friend from the group called, he was able to tell him, "George, I hate this, but I'm hanging in there."

"Hey, nobody promised you a rose garden! But listen: I just want you to know I've been praying for you, and I'll keep it up."

"Well — thanks; I guess I'd be a liar, if I said I didn't need it."

"Okay, I'll check with you tomorrow."

Mark was touched by that call and the care of his friends. All his life he had been a loner, proud of the fact that he didn't need anyone. Now he realized that he did, and he was grateful to God for the friends He had given him.

It took him the whole day and part of the early evening to fill out that report. The next day he tackled another, and the day after, another, and eventually he got caught up. But he didn't revert then; he got his reports in when they were due, and even occasionally got one in early. And a few months later, he noticed something extraordinary: he no longer hated doing them. God had answered his prayer and changed his heart about them. He didn't *like* doing them, but he no longer loathed it.

From time to time, my pastoral duties would take me past Mark's store, and I would drop in, to see how he was doing. "Hey," he said, laughing, "reports are never going to be my favorite thing, but I've got to admit, I like having my boss happy, when he calls." And Mark had given him good reason to be pleased. For God, in addition to changing Mark's attitude, had honored his obedience and blessed his endeavors. His store did turn a profit two years ahead of schedule; in fact, it remained profitable for the eight years that Mark was there, several years leading all the other stores in sales and profits.

The last entry in Mark's file recorded my most recent conversation with him. So impressed was the company with him, that they had turned over their largest store to him. It had slipped into the red, and they knew of no one in their organization who could do a better job of turning it around. That wasn't going to be easy, "But, hey," Mark concluded, chuckling, "I've learned one thing: nothing's impossible. Wasn't I turned around by a Master?"

7

JANE

Sometimes being a friend in Christ, requires putting that friendship in jeopardy. But the tougher the love, the greater the fruit it bears....

To look at Jane, no one would ever know that she had a care in the world. She and her husband Kirk were typical of the young couples who had moved into the attractive, growing suburb west of Rochester. And because of all the new split-level houses being built in the area, Parkminster Church was experiencing a boom.

Kirk and Jane had recently bought a house on a lovely birch-lined street that formed a secluded circle off one of the main roads. The house was spacious with four bedrooms, a patio, two-car garage, and all the latest appliances. They had started their family and were on their way to achieving all they had ever dreamed of.

As an engineer for Kodak, the big yellow giant of an industry in the area, Kirk was a 'comer.' Though still in his thirties, he had been promoted and was now managing a department. When their first child arrived, Jane gave up teaching high school, and now she was engrossed in everything that went on in the church.

My first serious encounter with this couple was at an evening meeting of the Christian education committee in their home. The issue to be decided that night was which curriculum to use, to teach high school students about dating and marriage. No sooner had the topic been introduced by the Christian Education director, than Jane expressed her opinion, emphatically and articulately. And she was obviously among friends, for she felt no hesitation about saying exactly what she thought.

My problem was that I felt exactly the opposite from Jane. Though I had been pastor of the church for several years, I had delegated this area of the program to the Christian Education director. How could I express my thoughts now, without offending Jane?

Well, I could not very well remain silent, and so, after several other members had spoken in agreement with Jane, I finally ventured my opinion. Immediately, Jane responded and with some force rebutted all my reasoning. I was caught by surprise. Seldom had anyone had the temerity (or openness) to challenge me.

After an awkward silence, the chairman tried to smooth things over, shifting the subject to a less volatile topic. Fortunately, the meeting ended soon after, and I went home as quickly as I could, making a mental note not to tangle with Jane again, if I could help it.

My next contact with her came almost six months later. The door of my office was open, and suddenly she stuck her head around the corner, grinning. "Guess what?" she almost shouted, "we're going to adopt a baby daughter. Kirk and I are going south next week to get her."

I was excited for them. Carol and I were the parents of four adopted children, and I well recalled the thrill for us, when we went to get each one of them. Maybe that was why Jane felt free to tell me; in any event, none of the estrangement of our previous encounter was present, as she hurried off down the hall to tell the women in the church office.

It must have been the wisdom of God that nudged Carol to invite Jane to be a member of the very first 3D group at church. Almost as soon as that happened, she began to warm up toward Carol and the others. And maybe our attitudes changed, too, for I was coming to realize that my strong opinions, though comfortable to me, were not always from the Lord, and often separated me from others, or at least scared them off. In that pilot 3D group, I had the responsibility of providing a ten-minute teaching at each meeting, and I believe this began to build a friendship with Jane, as she always seemed eager to listen to what was being said.

One afternoon, three months later, I was in my office with the door ajar, when Jane again looked in, this time hesitantly entering and staring at the floor, her face and neck red with embarrassment. She asked about how many reservations we had for the Presbytery dinner the next day, since she was in charge of cooking the meal, and I replied that we had 25 ministers coming. But I sensed that church business was not what had brought her into my office. Something else was troubling her, something personal. And apparently it was something she was uncomfortable about, so I didn't query her, but just waited.

Finally, she murmured, "You know I'm in the 3D group, don't you?" I nodded, but nothing more came. She grew more crimson. Then, she summoned up all her courage and asked, "Did Carol tell you what happened this morning?"

"No," I replied, "I haven't seen her yet."

By this time, Jane had slumped into a chair and was rubbing her hands. Seeing that this was really a professional visit, I came around from behind my desk, sitting opposite her and turning my note pad to a fresh page.

"Well," she said, talking to the floor, "you know I've just started my second 12-week session of 3D. After our meeting last night, your wife and the other leader asked if they could see me this morning."

Jane said that she could not imagine what they wanted to see her about, but was more curious than apprehensive — until she saw their faces, coming up the walk. This was not going to be a light, social visit. She welcomed them and gave them coffee, and after they had chatted a bit, Carol had come right to the point: "Jane has anyone ever told you, you have body odor?"

She was speaking so softly that Jane could hardly hear her. But she did hear her, and was speechless.

"How often do you shower?" Carol asked her.

Her first reaction was to tell her that it was none of her business and to leave the room. But it was obvious to her that this was not easy for the two co-leaders, either; in fact, after more than three months of caring fellowship in 3D, it was still extremely difficult for them. Finally, Jane told them that she had no regular schedule for showers. And then she wondered why, because she did have a schedule for practically everything else in her life. I smiled at that and made a note on my pad; Jane was the most incredibly well organized individual I had ever met.

She asked the co-leaders if they had any discernment as to why she had omitted scheduling showers, and they couldn't help her, suggesting only that she ask God, since He had already shown her much about herself in other areas. And then they came and gave her a big hug. There were tears in Jane's eyes, as she related their loving concern, and I marveled at the miracle of love which I had seen take place in her small group. Where else would anybody care enough to confront such a difficult subject? How many Christians in churches across the nation turned off others, because of unsuspected personal habits? How many close friends loved one another enough, to speak the truth which would set them free?

"Frankly," Jane went on, "that's really why I'm here. Ever since they came to see me, I've been trying to get a handle on it, and I can't. I thought maybe you could."

"I don't know," I replied. "But why don't you just start talking, and we'll see if the Holy Spirit will give us a clue."

Jane said she had been an achiever all her life. I believed that, for I could see how much of a do-er she was in church. She had an enormous capacity for taking on and accomplishing many things. Ask Jane to organize a women's luncheon for 200, and she would do it perfectly within a week. Ask her to take on the project of painting and decorating all the bathrooms in the church, and before I knew it, she would have crews of members working like beavers on a Saturday morning, until the project was completed. Nor did she ever do anything halfway or half-heartedly; everything was a first-class job. And beautifully scheduled — she could accomplish more in a given time frame than any three people I knew.

Jane continued with her personal inventory. She said that her mother had always stressed personal cleanliness; indeed, she herself showered every day. So why was this the one area Jane had fallen down? She looked at me, but I just shook my head and encouraged her to go on.

Jane talked about her appearance now. She had been very athletic in high school, and would have been in college had there been a sports program for women. In high school, she had played varsity field hockey and volleyball, and was captain of the basketball team. She was also an academic achiever, graduating cum laude and being named to the Phi Beta Kappa honor society. But since she married, she had put on too many pounds. She tried every possible way to reduce, but nothing seemed to work. After years of trying and failing, she said she had just given up. "Nothing I did would ever improve my appearance," she mused, "because I weighed so much. So why bother trying to make myself pretty and acceptable? After all, what I look like isn't important."

It was then, Jane said, that she had decided to concentrate on her house. After all, she rationalized, didn't God want her caring more about others than herself? She believed He wanted her to make her house acceptable to others. I made a note on my pad and just let her talk, to see if she would see it, too.

She did. Gradually, as she talked, I could see her brighten. "So," she said, like a detective in a movie, "instead of spending any time keeping myself neat and clean, I must have poured all my energy into my house — which I made into a showcase." She shook her head. "And I see now, the reason why we entertained so much: it was so I could show off my house. If I couldn't be accepted for my own appearance, at least I could be accepted for my home's appearance." She sighed and smiled. "And the problem was compounded, because I couldn't accept myself!"

It was a joy for me, to see Jane's joy, as she unraveled the mystery. "Of course God wants me to be neat and clean! Of course I am more important than my house! Of course more people will see me in the course of a week, than will ever see the house! How dumb I've been! When I gave up on my appearance, I *really* gave up!" She lapsed into silence now, thinking about what she had just seen.

"Tell me about how 3D fits into the picture," I said, familiar with 3D's use of the concept of voluntary self-discipline. It was a Scriptural principle, from Hebrews 12: "All discipline for the moment seems painful rather than pleasant, but afterwards it yields the peaceful fruit of righteousness, for those who are trained by it." Being overweight myself, I knew how necessary self-discipline was, but how would a discipline of shower-taking work?

Jane said that she had decided to take a shower at 9:30 every night, without fail. Since she did everything else according to a timetable, she would do this, too. How did she feel about it? Like all disciplines, it was a little scary to contemplate, but exciting too. She couldn't wait to get started.

Two weeks later, Jane stopped in, to tell me how things were going. "You know," she said thoughtfully, "a lot more is going on than just hygiene. That first shower on the new discipline was like a baptism — I felt like all my sins and wrong attitudes were being washed away. In the morning, dressing for the new day, I found myself deliberately picking a pretty dress to wear, instead of just pulling on whatever was handiest. I've been doing that, ever since, and putting on make-up, and taking care of my appearance."

I asked her, if she noticed any change in her attitude about herself, and she smiled. "Well, for one thing I'm discovering that I still do have some positive feelings about myself. And my group tells me that they can see quite a difference."

I did, too, I told her and thereafter made a point of complimenting her on her appearance, when she deserved it, which she always did.

Five more weeks passed, before Jane again knocked on my office door. I was deep in reading a commentary on the text of Sunday's sermon, but set it aside and invited her in. Right off, she told me that a fascinating thing had happened after the last meeting in my office. Easter was approaching, and in keeping with her new attention to her appearance, she wanted a new dress for the Easter Sunday service. But that meant clothes-shopping, and because of her size, she hated going from store to store, looking in the racks for the larger sizes, and constantly being reminded of her weight. Previously she invariably wound up picking out something drab and without style, which was all a part of her having given up on herself. This time, she decided to share her need of a new dress with her 3D group, and she asked them to pray for her. Lori, one of the members, offered to go with her and help her select a dress. She was grateful, because Lori had an obvious sense of style, and she had never had anyone go with her before.

The next day, Jane picked Lori up and arrived at Lord & Taylor's almost as soon as the doors opened. Jane headed for the department which carried the large dresses, but Lori reminded her that she had lost some weight on 3D; why didn't she try first in the regular dress department? Jane said she felt just like a little girl at Christmas, as for the first time in years, she was surrounded by racks and racks of dresses which might fit her.

After trying on many, many dresses, she finally saw one which looked rather plain, but made of a soft, feminine fabric. As she tried this one on, she knew it was the dress for Easter Sunday. Never had she worn such a beautiful dress! But, said Lori, they weren't going to stop there; she took Jane to look for just the right accessories, to set it off. And that was something that Jane had never done before, not even before she put the weight on. Lori helped her find a lovely white butterfly necklace and bracelet, to accent the dress, and Jane couldn't wait to get home and get all dressed up.

That night, while the children were still up, Jane quietly slipped away to her bedroom, took the new dress out of the bag, and put it on. Carefully, she added the butterfly jewelry, slipped on her best, white high heels and spent a lot of time, getting ready in front of the mirror. Then, very quietly, she descended the stairs and appeared before the family in the den.

Tears came to Jane's eyes, as she recalled what happened next. Kirk was stunned. His eyes glistened, as he told her that never had he seen her so beautiful! The children echoed Kirk's sentiments, wondering where she was going, looking so nice. She herself had started to cry. She cried and cried, and the tears would not stop coming. For the first time since she had been married, she felt acceptable to herself.

After she had made use of the ever-present box of kleenex on the lamp table, I asked her if she could sum up what she had learned from the past six weeks. "Well," she said, taking a deep breath, "I've learned that I can take on a new discipline, stick to it, and have it work for me. I've not been too good at sticking to any discipline for a sustained period." She laughed ruefully. "Follow through has not exactly been my strong suit, unless there was some strong ego-reward involved."

She turned and looked out the window. "It's really amazing what just being obedient to that shower-a-day routine has done in my life, how many other things it has affected! No wonder God says not to disparage the little things in life."

Was that the most important thing, then? She thought for a moment before replying. "No, it isn't. To be honest, I think it was the lesson of accepting an excruciating correction, realizing that it was not annihilation, to say nothing of rejection, and letting it work for me. I did not lose my relationship; on the contrary, we're even closer now than we were. They feel like sisters to me now. I feel so much freer; I'm not afraid to tell them *anything!* And what a gift from God that is!"

I nodded, at a loss for words. She had said it so well, anything I could say would be redundant.

8
JACKIE

Jesus came for the imperfect, but we tend to forget that....

Spring was Jackie's favorite season. And on this spring day, outside her Dutch Colonial house in Arlington, Massachusetts, the tulips and iris were poking up from under the ground, and the trees had a faint shimmer of new green leaves. Jackie was sitting in her lovely, large sewing room, working on comforters for the guest room and thinking that the house which she and her husband John had recently moved into was just perfect. Many young doctors, lawyers and business executives on their way up, lived in their neighborhood, and you could almost feel success and promise in the air.

Jackie began to daydream, mentally taking inventory of her situation. It all seemed so ideal: she was the mother of two quick, lovable children. Her husband was an up-and-coming geologist for a large company, and everyone said he had a bright future. She was only 33, and her dream of being successful was already fulfilled. What more could she ask for?

Yet Jackie had to admit to herself that she was feeling miserable. She sensed an emptiness inside of her; she felt unfulfilled and dissatisfied. But what else was there to achieve? The gnawing feeling of unease remained with her, and returned the next day more strongly, taking the luster off all of her accomplishments. Finally, she became so uncomfortable that she put aside her sewing and began to make a list of all the things that still needed doing around the house. It didn't help, and worst of all, she had to admit that this wasn't the first time she had felt that way. The uneasy, empty, miserable feeling had been with her from childhood, and periodically it rose to torment her.

I first met Jackie in Rochester, where she was a delegate to a 3D conference at our church. She was a petite, trim, dark-haired young woman with dark flashing eyes and a delightful English accent. She had a pretty face, but it was marred by the hard set of her jaw and the sense of drivenness which radiated from it. Suspecting that she possessed a strong will and an obsessive, compulsive personality, I was curious to learn her story. The opportunity came two days later, during a coffee break. We got to chatting, and she told me briefly what had happened to her, and how she was struggling to break out of her lifelong pattern.

Jackie was the second of four children in her family. Her sister was four years older than she, and her father was a career diplomat with the U.S. State Department. He had served in the foreign service for over 24 years and was often commended for the superior job he did at each assignment.

An excellent diplomat, her father was nonetheless a hard taskmaster, demanding the same excellence from his staff — and his family — that he demanded of himself. He had raised his children to excel, just as he had pushed himself. He worked constantly, never relaxing and meticulous about details, and expected the same attitude from his co-workers — and his family. He allowed himself one diversion: golf. But even here, he was obsessive, practicing at every opportunity, driving himself to win and to overcome.

So all-consuming was this drive, that he was filled with judgment of anyone who did not strive as hard as he did, and that went especially for members of his family and relatives. Dinner times would often be a time when her father would recite all that was wrong with the relatives. His sister, a nun, was a busybody; Uncle Eddie was a hypochondriac; Aunt Edna was a fool, and so on. Even Jackie's mother came in for ridicule. To little Jackie, the message was loud and clear: don't ever be a gossip, a hypochondriac, a fool. . . the list grew longer with each dinner.

By the time she was ten, Jackie had already lived in India, the Azores, where her father had been the American consul, and in Ireland, where he had been the consul under the American ambassador to Dublin. She liked Ireland the best, because she went to a convent school and was taught by nuns. She was a quick study, and without even trying, she was able to make all A's in her work. It was in the Catholic school that she formed her Christian beliefs and came close to God, as a child. She discovered a group of children in her neighborhood that she could play with, and filled those wonderful days with carefree activity.

Things began to change, when her family moved to Portugal, where her father was now the U.S. consul in Oporto, the second largest city in the country. They lived in a big house, surrounded by high walls and a wrought-iron fence, with 10-foot-high steel gates controlling the entrance to the property. There was little grass, and certainly no play yard for children. Six servants helped the family, as befitted the ranking American diplomat. One day, soon after arriving in Oporto, the family was dining in their new home, when her father addressed her from the head of the table: "Jackie, your mother and I only expect you to do the best you can. But you must do that." That remark triggered a panic reaction inside of her, and from that moment on, in everything she did, she ran as though her life depended on it. Indeed, her father's admonition was like a starter's gun at a track meet: she bolted out of the blocks, determined to win the race, whatever distance it was. And that drive, set in motion some twenty years before, had never ceased.

Jackie immersed herself in learning Portuguese, developing her skills in horseback riding, tennis, and swimming, all the while continuing to sail through the English school at her own accelerated pace. By 15, she had finished high school and had to fill in courses, until she was old enough for college.

But despite a straight-A academic record and success in all sports endeavors, things were not going well inside for Jackie. She laughed now, as she recalled for me those pressure-packed days. "I had a compulsion to be perfect. After all, if my parents wanted the best, then I would give it to them and make them happy." She accomplished this by setting seemingly impossible standards for herself. If she went horseback riding, she would pick out the best and most experienced rider and try to beat him. If she failed, she would sink into despair, even though he was older and so much more experienced that he naturally won. She remembered swimming with a boy in her school and beating him repeatedly, until he grew into his size. The moment she could no longer beat him, she stopped competing with him. For that was the reverse side of the coin: losing was intolerable. On the tennis court, if she knew she had no chance of beating her opponent, she would play halfheartedly; that way, she could tell herself that she lost, because she was not really trying.

As a teenager, Jackie's obsession for perfection — for by now, that's what it was: a full-blown obsession — shifted from sports to her appearance. She was never satisfied with the way she looked, feeling perpetually fat and ugly, and anxiously dieting to shed a few more pounds. She would compare herself with other girls, and if she thought she looked fatter, she would be in a blue funk for days. In her fat moods, she would try and hide her imagined weight under bulky sweaters. Conversely, when she felt good about herself, she would make herself a new outfit to highlight her appearance. In the summer, she was careful to maintain a good tan, and of course, she was anxious to attract the right kind of boys — the sort her father would approve of.

One day after school, Jackie came home not feeling well. She was obviously glum, and her mother, responding to her mood, blurted out, "Where has the good Jackie gone?" Jackie was devastated. How could she let her mother down like that? From then on, she always had to appear to be on top of things, even if inside she couldn't pull it off.

Another time she came home from school, having won an award for a class project. Neither of her parents gave her any recognition; it was *expected* that she would win the award. In fact, never did she hear them say, "Jackie, we are proud of you." And gradually she formed the impression that she belonged to a special family, for whom outstanding performance was the norm.

Life became an endless race, and every time she approached the finish line, someone would move the tape further down the track, and she would have to race on. And behind her, always threatening to overtake her, was the specter of failure. So on she ran, and if the thought ever flitted across her mind of just collapsing on the grass by the side of the track, she was haunted by the words of her father, ever ringing in her ears: "Jackie, we only expect you to do your best."

When it was time for her to go to college, it was her father who suggested that she go to Radcliffe. For his daughter, only the most academically demanding college would do. Besides, Radcliffe had a scholarship program for children of diplomats, and with her academic record, it was awarded to her — as expected.

College was a shock for Jackie. How would she ever manage in such an unstructured environment? What would she do without the daily unspoken urging of her father and mother? On her own for the first time in her life, Jackie found herself to be an emotional cripple. She had no desire to join in sports, even though in several she was by now extremely good. She participated in few extra-curricular activities and maintained no social life. Out from under the constant pressure of her parents to achieve, she felt lost and alone.

Academically, she had gone to college, intending to major in French, perhaps as a precursor to a foreign service career, but a freshman course in Geology whetted her appetite. She had taken no science courses at the English school in Portugal, and now, as the Geology professor introduced the class to paleontology and mineral geology, she became very excited; a whole new vista of learning opened before her eyes. And she loved the frequent field trips which took her to the great outdoors.

Up to this point, for the first time ever, she had not done well in her studies, but Geology changed all that. Now she had something to work for, a goal for the following three years that could drive her the way her parents had. It was through Geology that she met her future husband, another "rock-knocker" like herself. Actually, John was a brilliant doctoral student at Harvard, who intended to pursue Geology in the private sector.

Now, sitting in that sewing room in their house in Arlington, and reviewing her life, Jackie could see the evidence of her obsessive, compulsive behavior all around her. She had driven John to get this house, which had to be big and spacious, like her parents' house in Oporto. She had made a project of painting, decorating, and refurbishing it. After marriage, and John's graduation with a Ph.D., children arrived in quick succession. Andrew and Allison became projects for perfection, too.

Her obsession led to ever more bizarre behavior. She felt afraid to go out of doors. She was petrified, when she contemplated riding on the subway. She was deathly afraid that she might meet an acquaintance or college friend while walking down the street who would not remember her, so she was on the lookout constantly. If she saw such a person, she would quickly cross the street, or turn around and retrace her steps, so she wouldn't have to encounter them.

She became mildly paranoid, and then not so mildly. Afraid that, while outside, she might be mugged or beaten or raped, she came to view everyone passing her on the street as a potential assailant, and began to imagine that people were following her. It got to the point where she would demand that John protect her and do everything with her. He had to drive her to her teaching job every day, and pick her up every night. And since she could not bring herself to acknowledge that there might be anything wrong with her, she rationalized this behavior as a romantic desire for togetherness.

A couple of months before, Jackie had faced a new crisis. The family had been tobogganing on a Sunday afternoon. The snow that January was hard-packed and dry, particularly good for sledding. On one downhill run, John, who was on the back of the toboggan, was bumped off and badly hurt his knee. She had taken him to the hospital, only to find that he would have to have an operation for torn ligaments in his knee. She wanted to visit him daily, but was afraid to drive, having always relied on him for that. The next day, she forced herself at noon to walk down to the nearby subway stop, board the train, and get off at the proper stop, hurry up the stairs, and walk rapidly to the hospital. Up on the street, she almost ran to the hospital, because she felt someone was following her and would grab her at any moment. Each day for the next week, while he was recovering in the hospital, she followed the same routine. But on his first day home, while his leg was still in a cast, she insisted that he drive her to school, because she was afraid to go alone.

At the same time, she constantly criticized John. If she was perfect, he had to be also. He had to do everything her way, and even so, he seemed to always do things wrong. Sitting now, with the quilt in her lap, she could catch only a faint glimpse of the dreadful irony of that: she had determined that she would never make demands of anyone like her father did of her, but now she was behaving exactly like him. She recalled an incident in a restaurant, when John had ordered the wrong thing from the menu, and then compounded the wrong by calling the waiter, "sir". Appalled that her husband should be so socially ignorant, she set out to correct him in all that he did, and therefore help him to be a better person. And through his fear of her judgment, she was able to control him, for John would do anything to keep peace between them. Nor would she entertain any of his spontaneous ideas for fun things for them to do, since they didn't fit in with her plans for the day.

Her home was one place where perfection was possible, and Jackie threw herself into her housework with abandon. She cleaned and polished it, till it shone, and she thrived on the compliments about its beauty. The kitchen floor always had a high gloss on it, and if anyone spilled anything on it, she almost went berserk. She always had a long list of things to do — wash and wax the floor, clean the oven, wash the curtains, make a dress, redecorate a room — and, above all, keep perpetually busy. She had a compulsive drive to finish that list. But like the unknown track official who kept moving the finish line further down the track, no sooner did she scratch off more entries on the top of the list, than she added new ones to the bottom.

And because Jackie had to do it all herself, she eliminated those things that she couldn't do to perfection. For example, she and John would often invite friends over for a snack. But somehow, serving a snack didn't suit her, so she would increase the planned menu, until it encompassed a gourmet meal. Yet that took so much work and left the kitchen so messy, she eliminated having guests at all.

The place where Jackie's sickness showed up most was in her children. When Andrew was two years old, she took him outside one day to play in the yard, telling him not to touch the grass or flowers, because he would hurt them and get himself dirty. As she occupied herself by reading a book — after all, she couldn't waste time just sitting there and watching Andrew — she finally looked up and noticed her son, sitting with his arms folded across his chest. So anxious was he not to touch anything that he had decided the best thing to do was to keep his hands to himself. Her child, she thought, had to play perfectly.

When her daughter Allison was two, Jackie began to teach her how to play in a doll house. But Allison insisted on putting the doll bed in the living room. Irritated that her daughter was so stupid, Jackie patiently corrected her, showing her over and over that the bed belonged in the bedroom. When she had finished the lengthy lesson, she left her daughter to play, only to discover later that Allison had given up playing with the doll house, because it wasn't any fun.

If Andrew brought out toys to play with in the family room, Jackie made sure that he put back all the pieces, becoming almost frantic, when he would want to play with the set of little building blocks which had hundreds of pieces. Though she never actually forbade him, he got the unspoken message and after awhile never touched them, although they were once his favorite thing.

In short, both of her children had to be perfect — in play, and later, at school. After all, weren't they extensions of her? They had to eat neatly, stay clean and tidy, be polite, and achieve top marks in school. She had little concern for how they felt inside, or what their needs were, as long as they looked good.

By this time, Jackie and John had joined a local Presbyterian Church, located in a heavily built up area of Cambridge. An old church, it was fixed up and refurbished as best it could be by the caring members, and though at first Jackie and John kept to themselves, very soon they were drawn into the active fellowship of the young couples. It wasn't long before both of them were elected deacons. This meant that Jackie, who was no longer teaching during the day, would be included in a Friday morning sharing group for other women deacons and the wives of elders.

A dozen women gathered weekly for prayer, Bible study, and sharing about their needs, and Jackie was petrified at the prospect. She had never had a close relationship with anyone other than her husband, and she was not about to share any problems, even if she could find some. Quickly she volunteered her house as a meeting place. She wanted the other women to see her pretty home, and besides, if she was the hostess, that would give her something to do, and she wouldn't be forced to relate with the group members.

For the first six months she was in the group, Jackie shared very little. After all, she told herself, she was not there because she had chosen to be in the group, but because she was a deacon. In the beginning, the problems the other women would share seemed superficial and unimportant to her. Yet she was also meeting some of these women through other activities at the church, and they were becoming friends. Gradually, after listening to the others for a long time, she began to identify with the needs they were sharing. She found herself wanting to confide in them, and to hear what the Holy Spirit might say through them, but opening her mouth was a major battle.

Finally, one Friday, after eight months of meeting every week, she heard a pause in the group discussion, and rather timidly, in her prim English accent, she mentioned a problem she was having with her weight. Though she weighed only 115, she still saw herself as fat and ugly, just as she had during her teen years in Portugal. To her surprise, none of the others saw her that way; in fact, they began to talk to her about her distorted image of herself. She listened, and couldn't believe that eleven other intelligent, perceptive women couldn't see what she saw about herself. Finally she had to accept what they were saying and agreed not to ever say that about herself again.

After a year, eight of the women who were young mothers, decided to also meet on Wednesday mornings, to help each other in raising their children, as there was not enough time on Fridays, if they included all their parental problems. In addition, they had heard about a

3D mothers group format, which they thought would meet their needs. Among other things, it recommended giving each mother a turn at caring for all the children in the church nursery, while the rest of the mothers met in the social hall outside the nursery and kitchen, to share their needs which concerned their children.

Their first Wednesday was a pleasant morning in July, and all eight of the mothers, including Jackie, were present — or rather seven were, as Janet had been given first turn at being in charge of the children. After praying for the Lord to teach them that day, Jill, who had left a promising career as a mechanical engineer, said to Jackie, "You know, I've noticed that Andrew never gets dirty. I had him last week in the Sunday school nursery, and he was afraid to play with the other children. I couldn't figure it out, and then it dawned on me that he was afraid to get himself messy! I knew it, when I gave him finger paints to play with, and he almost froze: he was afraid they might leave marks on his hands or clothes. What's wrong with him?"

The words hit Jackie like a bolt of lightning. *Wrong with him? Nothing could be wrong with one of her children!* She became immediately defensive; someone was saying she had not raised them perfectly. "He doesn't really like finger paints," she declared with assurance. "He doesn't like to play with messy things. He enjoys playing with detailed toys, and even a calculator." But the others in the group supported Jill's observations, and finally Jackie nodded her head in assent, not really agreeing but just so their attention would shift from her to someone else.

Thinking about it later, she acknowledged to herself that Andrew had always been quick in his responses, even as a baby. He learned to talk earlier than any other children she had known. And as he seemed like a quiet child, so she had encouraged him to enjoy books and passive pleasures. But now, recalling Jill's observation, she knew it was true. And that petrified her: that others in the group could see her child's problems more clearly than she could. "I wanted to run and hide," she would tell me later, "I wanted to take Andrew to a doctor right then and get him fixed up. My child had to be perfect!"

Slowly, as the weeks went by, Jackie came to see that she really needed to hear what the other mothers were trying to show her about her children. But she had so convinced herself that her children were exactly the way she wanted them to be, that she had to plead with God to help her believe what they were saying. At home, she would ask the Lord to show her the truth about her children, and gradually she began to see the harm she was doing to them — and in retrospect, what her father had done to her. Because they were almost the same.

After several more weeks, she finally accepted that her friends, who were Christians like herself, were only saying to her and trying to show her what they felt that God Himself wanted them to say, and her to see. And as she began to accept by faith that they were His instruments, imperfect as they were, her attitude began to change. Her friends continued to be loving and kind, but they would not let her escape the reality that her drive for perfection had poisoned her whole family. Ever so slowly her eyes began to open, until she, too, began to catch glimpses of what the others saw — and what God had been wanting her to see, for so long.

Three weeks later, it was Jackie's turn to watch the children, while the others met. She kept a close eye on Andrew — and was struck at the way in which he refused to play with the other children, if he sensed he would get messed up. Suddenly the full truth of all that her friends had been saying to her hit her like a gigantic sledge hammer. She had to do something.

Jackie decided that she had to change her way of raising her son, and as she had always relied on the strength of her will to make things happen, in this, too, she applied her determination. On their way home, she bought Andrew some finger paints, and in the kitchen watched, gritting her teeth the whole time, while he enjoyed the squishy feeling of the paints between his fingers — and on almost all of his clothes. Next, she persuaded John to build the children a sandbox, where they could grub and dig around as much as they pleased. She took Andrew and Allison to the playground, where she spent what seemed like hours, pushing their swings — an activity which seemed totally unproductive. Nevertheless, she kept it up for as long as they called for more, though it seemed their appetite was endless.

The hardest thing of all was inviting several of the other mothers to visit her at home and bring their children. Inside her head, she went crazy and almost became physically ill at the sight of all those children romping and playing in her neat, clean house.

And where was John in all this? By this time he, too, had seen the truth that Jackie's friends were speaking, and when she asked him to help her break the deadly pattern of obsessive control, he agreed, promising to tell her whenever he sensed she was getting into it. When they next went to a restaurant, he decided on where they would sit. Jackie had all she could do not to butt in and correct him. At other times, when he refused her directions, she would respond that she was only making a suggestion. The more this happened, the more she realized what a grip her drive for perfection had on her. Yet when they started to redecorate the bathroom together, she couldn't help taking charge, justifying her action by saying that she really did know how to hang the wallpaper better than he did. But she also knew God wanted her to change, and so she asked for His help daily, and set her will to give up the control of her children and her husband, every time she had the choice. When she failed, she confessed to the Lord and told her group — and resolutely started all over again. And slowly, but perceptibly she changed.

The final obsession which had to be dealt with was her house. For many years John and Jackie had been visiting the Community of Jesus on Cape Cod for retreats, vacations, and various meetings. They had often heard the Community directors speak, and knew they would benefit in their married life together, from the truth Cay and Judy spoke. They were drawn to the life in Christ they found at the Community, and Jackie especially felt great waves of freedom wash over her, every time she was there. She would often talk to John about moving to the Cape, when he retired, to be a part of the life and freedom of the Community.

One day, she heard of a house for sale, adjacent to the Community itself. The very next weekend, she drove down with her husband and another couple, who were friends from church and had shared some of their visits to the Cape. The four of them saw the house, fell in love with it, and decided to buy it on the spot. Before they knew it, they were talking like giddy school children about moving down and moving in. For the men, it would be a difficult but not impossible commute, and for Jackie, it would mean being freed from the Arlington house, which had become like an albatross round her neck, dragging her down.

On the drive back, she could hardly believe what they had done. It was so unlike her to do such an impulsive thing. It was not a part of her plan — in fact, it was not part of any plan. She had never felt so out of control — but it felt good, deliciously good! God was at the helm, and whatever way He took their ship now, that was fine with her. Besides, looking back, there was no denying that He was an infinitely better helmsman than she was.

After meeting Jackie at the 3D conference, I had made a note to follow up and find out whether she was being healed of her obsessions. And indeed, our paths continued to cross over the years. The last time I saw her was a few weeks ago, when I had visited them at their new Cape Cod home. She still spoke with her lovely English accent, but she was so incredibly free that it was hard to believe she was the same person. As we were chatting, Andrew came in from playing outside, covered with dirt from head to toe. He, and his sister who followed him in the door, appeared full of life and without any signs of stress and strain.

Once again, God had healed — and released a family from a bondage that at first they had not even recognized.

9

BETH

Fantasy or reality? Choosing the latter is always more painful, but it is ultimately more joyful. . . .

I was a teenager, attending a local Presbyterian Church in northwest Washington D.C. with my family, when I first met Beth. She was six years younger than me, but her age group and mine were sometimes combined for youth activities. Not that I cared, for at that age I certainly had no interest in associating with anyone so young.

Thirty years later, Carol and I were attending a clergy couples retreat at the Community of Jesus, when a small blond woman came up and identified herself as Beth from Washington. I drew a blank at first, and then it came back — the brick church on the corner, the Wednesday youth dinners, dozens of singspirations, and little Beth tagging along with her older brothers and sister. Later that afternoon, during some free time, we got together, and I heard the incredible story of Beth's fight for reality, which she was just then winning.

On the morning of Ash Wednesday several years before, Beth was cleaning the downstairs bathroom of the home where she was staying for six weeks. A minister's wife for 15 years, she had endured continued stress, until she felt she was about to have a nervous breakdown. The one place which had given her a measure of peace in the past was also able to provide 24-hour residential care for those in need of spiritual healing and growth. She had asked to go there and was accepted, and was now living in one of the Community homes.

It was a large house with natural wooden shingles — a more beautiful house than any she had ever lived in. The downstairs bathroom was long and narrow, with a dark wood wainscoat and bright flowered paper. Beth's room was right next door, but she could not appreciate the beauty of her surroundings. Pressures had been building up in her for a long time, until she felt ready to explode. She felt stomach pains continually, and inside, she felt in constant turmoil. This morning, it was her turn to clean the bathroom, and opening the cabinet under the bathroom sink, Beth spied a bottle of liquid cleaner. Impulsively, she took a paper cup from the dispenser next to the sink and filled it. Placing it carefully on the counter, she filled another cup and put it beside the first. Then she carefully screwed the cap on the bottle and replaced it.

Almost ritualistically, she gulped down the contents of first one cup and then the other. Was she consciously trying to take her life? On one level, yes; on another, deeper level, no, for she could see that there was no skull and crossbones warning on the label. What *was* going through her mind at that moment was that the acrid, pungent liquid would help her float free in space, totally alone, without anyone else to intrude, while escaping her uncomfortable inner feelings. It was a desire she had secretly had for some time, and now it would become a reality.

Continuing to wipe off the mirror and straighten the towels on the rack, she waited for something to happen to her. She was scared of what might happen, but she was consumed with the need to get in control of her life, which seemed to be falling apart — at least, in enough control to escape from the pain of it. She monitored her pulse, as she had been taught in nursing school, waiting for some sense of fainting or blackness, but nothing happened.

Beth left the bathroom, and putting away her cleaning materials, readied herself along with the other members of the household, to attend the service in the chapel down the street, which marked the beginning of Lent. Sitting in church, she had almost forgotten her rash behavior of half an hour before, when suddenly she felt pains in her stomach and started to vomit. Someone from her house helped her out of the chapel and back to her room, while another friend called the doctor. By this time, Beth was vomiting severely and experiencing extreme diarrhea.

When the doctor arrived, he sat down beside her bed and examined her. After a long time, he looked puzzled, and said, "I can't figure out what caused this sudden attack you've experienced." Then he looked at her and gently asked, "Do you have any idea what caused it?"

Almost in a whisper, she answered, "I drank two cups of liquid cleaner."

That moment became the turning point of Beth's life. Somehow, hearing herself admit out loud to another person for the first time, the craziness that went on perpetually in her head and which had led to destructive thoughts and behavior, brought her into reality — and into accepting her great need of healing.

Beth was the youngest of seven children. Her father was the director of a rescue mission in the slums of Washington, D.C., and they lived in a nice five-bedroom apartment on the mission's top floor. On the corner of the building hung a neon sign which read, "Gospel Mission, Jesus Saves." Living in the run-down section of town was scary for Beth, and growing up, she was continually afraid. One evening when she was seven, she went down the five flights of stairs from their apartment to the street. As she started down the final steps, she saw a man's hand lying across the bottom step. Thinking it was her father, she screamed, and only calmed down when he came out of a meeting on the first floor of the mission and held onto her for a long time. Later, she could see that the hand was attached to a drunk who had fallen beside the bottom stair and was asleep.

So frightened was Beth that her body began to swell as a reaction to the panic, and it remained that way for several days. It was not uncommon for members of the family to find drunks in the laundry room, the hall closet, or other small places where they could sleep in warmth. Several times Beth would wake up at night, after having been asleep for several hours, and look out her bedroom door to see a derelict walking down the hall. Often, her sleep would be rudely interrupted by fights in the street below her window, or by the sirens of ambulances or fire engines, answering some emergency call nearby.

Living in that environment, surrounded by alcoholics, vagrants, and street people, and witnessing a number of shootings, knifings and rapes, left Beth in a state of persistent fear and a desire to be protected. Her living situation also left Beth with a feeling of isolation from the rest of the children her age. Her friends from church didn't want to come to her home, because of its location, and on one occasion in a church group, she was mortified, when a woman identified the dress Beth was wearing as having once belonged to her daughter, before it had been given to the church goodwill shop.

Even her father was an embarrassment to her. Every once in a while, during the middle of the pastor's sermon, he would let go with a loud "Amen!" He seemed unable to converse in normal tones but always spoke in his projecting voice and was not like the other fathers at the church. Neither was the mission's station wagon, which they came to church in. On its sides, her father had painted in large blue letters:

**Good News: Christ Came To Save Sinners
He Died and Rose Again**

Beth's church emphasized the Bible and missions. All during Sunday School, Wednesday school, or Vacation Bible School, she was taught to read and memorize the Bible. Her parents valued memorizing Scripture verses and verbalizing personal faith correctly, so Beth complied to gain acceptance. She felt secure in her religious beliefs, knowing that what she was being taught was right, even though other religious people might be wrong. She learned much about Jesus, and prayed when appropriate, but she lacked a personal, intimate relationship with her Saviour.

Aware of the effect Beth's environment was having on her, her parents arranged to have her go to Christian boarding schools in New Jersey and Illinois, during her high school years. She was small for her age, and immature, and she felt lonely and out of place in these schools — a feeling that was to stay with her for most of her life. Following high school, she enrolled in a Christian college to pursue a nursing career, but before she graduated at 22, she met and married her husband, Charlie, who felt called to the ministry.

While Beth was pregnant with her second child, and caring for her eight-month old son, her life became hectic and full of stress. Charlie was in school full-time now, preparing for the ministry, and since they had no money to live on, she worked in a veteran's hospital, 30 miles from their home. She began to suffer internal physical distress, for which her obstetrician could not find a cause, and sent her to a specialist. It continued after her daughter was born and, in fact, got worse; she lost 65 pounds in three months. After an extensive examination, the internist diagnosed her as having ulcerative colitis, and from her nurse's training, Beth knew that her illness had been brought on by emotional stress.

For the next nine months, Beth was in and out of the hospital, as the doctor tried transfusions, cortisone shots, and drugs to heal her. Nothing helped, so she was hospitalized for a total colostomy operation. For the next three years, she remained sickly and underwent several operations. She had a long history of internal bleeding, and again from her training, she knew that she would die, if she didn't heal. But slowly growing inside of her was an iron determination to live until her children grew up. Once they had reached adulthood, if she died, it didn't matter.

Life grew increasingly difficult for Beth, over the next ten years. She was often depressed about what she perceived as her poor care of her family, and she cried easily and often. Ever since her teen years, she had felt worthless and hated herself intensely. Looking around her, she saw everyone as socially more acceptable than she.

When her depression became more than she could bear, she went to her doctor, and he gave her Ridilin to elevate her mood, saying to her, "Beth, everyone needs a crutch once in awhile, to be able to function." The medicine did help for awhile, but her depression only returned with more severity than before. She found herself compulsively clinging to her children for security, and experiencing vast mood swings. From time to time, she would go back to her doctor for more medicine, but nothing seemed to stabilize her for long.

Beth's consuming passion was for her children, and she lived in constant fear that something bad would happen to them. Memories of living at the mission in her childhood added to her fears, and she was tormented by the possibility that someone would molest them or kidnap them. Her obsession about their safety led her to be with them constantly, and go with them everywhere. She was their companion on outings, recreation, errands, and any other activity which took them outside the house. Moreover, she continued this behavior, until her son was 17 and her daughter 16, yet the more she hovered over them, the more fearful she became.

Needless to say, her children increasingly resented her, and their response added to the tension she felt. It got to the point where she never felt stable or secure in anything, even in her marriage. Charlie chose to be passive and unaware of her worries. He never acknowledged that they had any problems, even though there was never enough money, as he would grow restless every three or four years and would take a new job, and they would have to move.

When the children became older, she tried working again, to bring in more income and find some security, but nothing really helped. She never experienced any periods of serenity or peace. More and more, Beth withdrew from the painful reality around her, finding solace in being alone and playing solitaire. Meanwhile, Charlie was so involved with his church work that he had little time for her or their children. It seemed to her that the whole weight of the family rested on her shoulders.

When a friend of Beth's suggested one day that she and Charlie attend a four-day clergy couples retreat at the Community of Jesus on Cape Cod, Beth was happy to agree. She wanted a respite from the tension around her. She had attended some retreats before, and they had been good experiences for her, and while she knew nothing of the Community, she respected her friend's judgment and obtained her husband's commitment that he would go with her.

After arriving for the retreat, Beth was surrounded by other couples who seemed to handle the problems of life a little differently than she did. When she heard other couples sharing with unusual candor in the meetings, she alternated between thinking that they were all weird, or speculating that she was the crazy one. Her old feeling of being less than others quickly returned.

The clergy and their spouses all talked quite openly about their feelings and needs. She had never been in a meeting where she was encouraged to express what was really going on in her head and in her feelings. It seemed foreign to her and somewhat scary, although she longed to share all the jumbled thoughts that were stored up there. But, deep inside, Beth felt a strong conviction that the other retreatants' way was right, straight, and true to the Bible.

By the third day of the retreat, Beth was feeling increasingly uncomfortable with the reality that she was beginning to see around her. She missed her children and felt unneeded as a mother. Realizing that she was not thinking at all clearly, she left the retreat meeting, and went and lay down on her bed in the retreat dorm. After awhile, she got up, and taking her toilet kit into the bathroom, she opened the half-full bottle of aspirin in it, gulped down the pills in it, and took a large drink of water.

What was her intent on this earlier occasion? Was it truly to take her life? If so, there were was a full bottle of sleeping pills in her suitcase, and if she could count on not being disturbed, they would have done the job. No, as she later related this episode to me, it seemed to me that she was flirting with the idea of suicide, the ultimate escape. Her children were still too important to her, to take permanent leave of them. So she acted out her favorite fantasy....

Someone entered the dorm room, so she stayed in the bathroom until they left. And then she had an unpleasant thought: "If I die, I will be in a state of limbo for eternity, and be alone with myself. Nobody else will be around." That frightened her; as much as she wanted to escape reality, she did not want to, at that cost.

Meanwhile the aspirins were taking effect. Her heart started pounding, and her pulse rate increased. She felt sick inside, but determined to return to the retreat, without telling anyone what she had done. She went back, and was somehow able to keep from being sick or drawing attention to herself, and after a couple of hours, she was more or less back to normal. Those meetings had a strange effect on Beth. Others would share about current problems in their lives, and Beth would be reminded of something totally unrelated in her past. But she was no longer silent; she would voice whatever she was thinking to the group, even though it bore no relation to where the spirit of the retreat seemed to be moving. Since there seemed to be no connection with the current conversation, the group would continue on after her interruption.

At the end of the retreat, the leaders urged Beth to seek additional help, as soon as she could. And she agreed, shaken by the realization that she had impulsively ingested a large amount of aspirin, the day before. That was aspirin — what might she take, the next time?

After returning home, Beth soon felt more panicky than ever, about her situation. Charlie was totally involved in a struggling ministry which included directing a Christian school and a community church, and as always there was precious little money coming in. She told Charlie, she didn't think the ministry was helping anyone, but he argued just the opposite, and meanwhile their children were exerting their independence and showing less and less need of her.

One evening it all came to a head, as she and Charlie argued about the value and future of the ministry. At the end of his rope, Charlie finally said, "Beth, either you leave, or I will, because we can't go on any longer like this."

Feeling rejected and unacceptable once again, Beth replied, "Okay, I'll leave. I'll see if I can go to the Community of Jesus, for a few weeks." Charlie agreed, hopeful that his wife might be able to get some help, and relieved that their incessant bickering would be over for awhile. She, too, hated the conflict between them — in fact, all her life Beth had feared any kind of conflict. As a little girl, she had seen the bouncers at the mission who had to bodily eject derelicts who became too noisy or disruptive. It was not a pretty sight. By contrast, her parents never said a cross word to each other. But when she and Charlie got married, it seemed like they fought over almost everything. She hated those times, and would withdraw rather than continue an argument. She simply did not know how to handle such a situation. When anyone said anything to her that made her face something real that she didn't like, she would retreat into fantasy and unreality. And now, rather than face any further conflict with her husband, she chose to leave.

She flew off to Cape Cod, half moved to get even with her husband, and half yearning for the security and the stability that the community there seemed to offer. When she arrived and was assigned to one of the homes, she was extremely reticent, afraid to share her dark and ugly thoughts with anyone, for fear they would think her mad. She remembered her mother telling her about her father being sent to a psychiatric ward before she was born, because he was writing postcards to Senators, inviting them to accept Jesus. That story had taught her to trust no one. She already felt unacceptable to herself and surely if anyone else knew her innermost thoughts, they might try to send her to some psychiatric ward, too.

She continued to indulge herself in intermittent fantasies about suicide. She imagined herself walking slowly out into the nearby bay, and as the water closed over her head, drowning. She imagined herself picking up a brick and smashing her head. She decided not to think about hanging herself, since that was probably awfully painful, however brief the pain. She thought, instead, of drinking something poisonous. Of course, she was careful not to tell anyone in her house about such thoughts, for if they knew, they would surely send her home.

And so, she continually drifted off into fantasy — just as she had, all her life. It was the surest way to avoid the painful reality around her. As a child, she would escape the threatening surroundings of the mission by creating a new, pleasant, controllable reality in her head. Later on, she would avoid the constant feeling of rejection and worthlessness by creating new worlds in her mind. In them, she could be anyone she wanted to be. She could shut out the stress of her marriage, children and job by going off alone with her thoughts. But when she was forced to live in reality, she didn't know how to make the switch. And she had to go back and forth so often, the boundaries between fantasy and reality became blurred. And because it was all so confusing, she welcomed suicide, as a way to peace.

That fateful Ash Wednesday, Beth was astonished at how easily she told the doctor of her suicide attempt. She had never shared that sort of thing with anyone before. About four months prior to her attempt, she had thought about suicide for a whole evening. The next day she had worked up enough courage to tell her pastor, but he had dismissed it as unimportant.

Beth now took the medication the doctor prescribed, then rested for a while. When she awoke, she went into the dining room, where the of the household members were eating supper. They had to be alarmed at her behavior and concerned for her safety, yet no one seemed to reject her; in fact, they were acting as if it had never happened. Beth couldn't believe it. She had done a terrible thing in their home, and no one shunned her or wanted her to leave.

The man who was the head of the household said, "We need to tell Charlie about this." Beth was startled for a moment; she had half-expected him to tell her she must pack and go home. But when he mentioned telling her husband, she hesitated; Charlie had never known about the crazy thoughts that swirled around her head. What would he do when he found out? Nevertheless, she quickly agreed, especially if it meant that she could stay. She felt so secure now among her new friends that she was willing to risk allowing her husband to see her craziness.

Charlie was to come the next afternoon, and Beth waited nervously for his arrival. He had never been involved in her problems before, and she sensed that he didn't want to be now. She was afraid to tell him all that she thought or felt. When Charlie arrived at the house, Beth tensed up and wanted to run, to escape the pain of reality. Soon, with the encouragement and support of the people in the house, she was able to sit and tell him all that had happened. He seemed to be able to take it and not reject her. And Beth, by choosing to expose herself so openly to her husband, felt that she had made a commitment to go on in her quest for healing.

Charlie returned home, and Beth continued her extended visit. At first, she expected that every day someone would tell her she had to go home. But that never happened. She never felt one moment of rejection from anyone in the house. She felt secure, when members of the house now spent more time with her, so that she would not be alone with her thoughts for long periods during the day. They genuinely seemed to care, and that was a new experience for Beth. Ever since she was a little girl at the mission, she had wanted to be protected, but no one had ever offered to keep her safe. Now she felt protected from the world, and mostly from herself.

As a mother, she had spent her life trying to protect her children from imagined dangers. Now she was the recipient for that kind of care, and it felt good. Speaking of her children, she missed them greatly during this period, and often felt the urge to go home, but inwardly she knew that they didn't need her, and that she had to let them go. Her whole life had been tied up with her children; they had been her reason for living. But now she had to find a new reason for going on. And that reason had to be Jesus.

During the weeks that followed, Beth would take long daily walks with Kathryn, one of the residents in her house. Kathryn had been through many traumas in her own life and had raised four children herself, yet she seemed so stable. Now Beth felt the beginning of trust and would share absolutely everything she was feeling and thinking, as they took their daily strolls. She felt she owed it to the Lord and to her new friends who had so lovingly accepted her, in spite of her behavior. Kathryn was the first person in all Beth's life who had cared enough to really listen to her, and take her thoughts and feelings seriously. Beth felt relieved to pour out her whole life history to Kathryn during those walks. All her hurts and hopes, all her dreams and disappointments, all her fantasies and failures, came tumbling out. And as this process continued, the craziness and emotional pressure in her head gradually subsided.

On one of their walks a month later, Beth was talking about her past, rehashing some of the things she had done. Abruptly, Kathryn interrupted her. "Beth, I don't know whether this is from the Lord, but you don't need to think or worry or talk anymore about your past. The time for that is over. You now need to live with all your energy and attention in the present."

Beth heaved a huge sigh of relief. Feeling as though a million pounds had been lifted from her shoulders, she began to relax and enjoy life. Nothing depended on her; things would go on perfectly well in the world without her. What a relief! For the first time in her 42 years, she felt free.

Beth had been at the Community six weeks already, and was trying to decide how long to stay, when on another walk she started talking about her teenage children and how much she missed them. Kathryn again spoke strong truth to her: "At this point, Beth, you need to face reality here, and not daydream about your children. It's unhealthy for you to spend so much time in your head, fantasizing."

Beth was furious! And when they arrived back at the house, Kathryn left her, to do an errand. All the memories of rejection, disapproval, and abandonment swooped down on Beth, to devour her. "Well, here's the rejection I've been expecting all along," she thought. "Kathryn wants me to leave."

She contemplated packing her bags and leaving that instant. But where would she go? Her obsessive hold on her family, a bondage which she had maintained for 20 years for her security, had been loosened. And she had gained enough understanding of herself to recognize that the compulsion she was feeling now had always been her pattern — to escape from reality. But what she was feeling was so powerful. . . . Next she thought about pills; maybe she would just take an overdose of whatever she could find around the house. It would be such a relief to just slide out of this agony — *no*! She had to choose between reality and fantasy, once and for all! Was she going to revert to the comfort of never-never land? Or was she going to choose to live in the reality of what Kathryn had spoken to her?

While she was at the crossroads of indecision, someone else in the house, sensing this, suggested that she go to her room and ask Jesus to help her choose. She did, and while praying by her bed, she decided to face reality and resist the temptation to retreat into the past and into unreality. She didn't know whether Kathryn would accept or reject her, but she decided to go on with Jesus, regardless.

Of course, Kathryn had nothing but love for her the next day, and in another week Beth felt that it was time for her to go home. She knew she wasn't entirely healed, but she felt confident and secure enough to leave and to function as a wife and mother again. Charlie had come to get her, and it gave Beth an opportunity to drive home with him and share all she had learned about herself.

Once home, it was difficult for Beth to adjust. She had to constantly release her grown children from her inordinate grasp, and she had to force herself to live in the present. Sometimes she thought she wouldn't be able to live another day, and she despaired of ever getting well. She couldn't seem to think a thought through to its end, and her mind sometimes seemed disconnected from her body. She even guessed, wrongly, that she was schizoid. The battle between fantasy and reality raged on, as Satan tried to reclaim her mind, but she called on Jesus and carried on with her life as best she could, with the aid of prayer and long-distance support from her new friends.

Two months at home was long enough for Beth. Charlie had promised her in April, that he and the children would spend two months with her at the Community during the summer. So the family packed the gray Chevy station wagon to the roof and drove off just before the fourth of July. As soon as they arrived, Beth noticed how peaceful she felt. No more were her thoughts disconnected. She felt secure. And best of all, she didn't have to perform as a mother or a minister's wife for two months. For the next eight weeks she relaxed and soaked up the stable, secure atmosphere all around her.

During those weeks she was often confronted with reality about herself or her circumstances. She always felt initially that the confrontation represented rejection from the person speaking it, but gradually she learned to listen and ask Jesus to help her hear the truth.

The most encouraging thing was, she could sense the healing going on inside of her. Charlie could see it, too; no longer was she so scattered and detached. She knew she had a long way to go, but she was well along the road, and it felt good.

During the next year, Beth began to develop a new relationship with her children and began to feel like a whole person. The following summer they all returned to the Community, and one balmy evening, she was walking down the small paved road in front of the home where she was staying. She and Charlie were just returning from the Community's Monday night teaching meeting. It was July, and the night air was fresh and filled with the smell of honeysuckle. Suddenly she thought, "This is a real place on planet Earth! It is not a dream! These are real people I am walking with!" It was the first time in her life she had ever reached out and touched reality.

She had finally, totally broken through the fog of unreality and fantasy which had enshrouded her from childhood. She had wrapped it around her early in life to protect her from the harsh and brutal reality of her life at the mission. Now for the first time she could discard that cloak of unreality. She could choose to stand on the rock of reality which was all around her. Her healing was taking place.

10

LOUIS

It's awfully hard to believe that sometimes the hardest things in our path are placed there by a loving God....

It is possible that our willingness to say things which we don't want to say, but which we know are the truth, may make the difference between life and death. It did in the case of a fellow pastor and a personal friend of mine, Louis....

October 16 was a beautiful Sunday in central Pennsylvania; the leaves were turning vibrant colors of rust, orange, yellow and red. Louis had lived there for 13 years, and he loved the area and the congregation he served. His church was located on Queen Street in the middle of a small, friendly town. It was an old brick two-story building, erected in 1844. The trim was white, the windows were made of stained glass, and the bell tower reached toward heaven, tolling at the beginning of each service.

I had known Louis for a long time. We met at a clergy retreat, and had gotten together monthly with our wives, to share common problems and joys. We also both enjoyed playing tennis, though we were both intensely competitive.

That Sunday was even busier for him, than most Sundays. He had been invited to preach at a nearby

Lutheran church for their early morning service, after which he would hurry back to teach an adult Sunday school class before preaching at the regular 10:15 a.m. service. It was at the end of the Sunday school class that Louis felt a twinge in the back of his head. Then his left arm and whole side suddenly became weak, as though someone had drained all the strength right out of them. A momentary flash of fear went through him. "What's happening to me?" he wondered aloud. "I don't know whether I'll be able to preach at the next service."

Quickly he ended his teaching and hurried upstairs to where the sanctuary was located, to get ready for the morning service which would begin in 15 minutes. Climbing the stairs, he spotted an elder and told him that he was not feeling well, asking him to take the service, and he would limit himself to preaching the sermon. When his wife, Dot, saw him she grew alarmed and cautioned him to take it easy.

By the time Louis was ready to preach, the twinge in his head had disappeared. But the weakness in his left side was still there. He took his place behind the marble pulpit, as he had done every Sunday for the past 13 years. He was proud of the fact that he had never missed a Sunday service, because of sickness. This had been home for Louis, ever since he graduated from seminary. He felt comfortable and safe here — but now he faced an intrusion: what was happening to him?

He managed to finish his sermon and cheerfully greet the people as they left, but back home the weakness was still with him. As he was scheduled to conduct a service of dedication for 12 couples who were renewing their marriage vows that evening, he decided to spend the afternoon resting. Dot said to him, "If you don't feel any better tomorrow, you're going to see the doctor." She was obviously worried. So was he, but he didn't tell her. What could she do anyhow, he thought? If I tell her about my own anxiety, that will only make her feel worse.

He felt better after resting all afternoon — well enough to go back to the church to fulfill his evening commitment. But it still bothered Louis that he couldn't figure out what was going on in his body. He had been to see an ophthalmologist just last week, and the latter had found some hemorrhaging in one eye and had tested him for diabetes. Maybe this had something to do with that....

That night, he slept well and woke up the next morning, expecting the weakness to have disappeared. But it hadn't. So after breakfast, at Dot's insistence, he called their local doctor and made an appointment to see him right after lunch. And at the appointed time, he made the familiar drive from his house to the church, a mile away, where Dr. Samad had his office in a converted storefront building which happened to be right next to the church.

Louis had not met this new doctor in town. His old doctor had retired and turned over his practice to Dr. Samad, and as Louis had not had a checkup for two years, he was entering the office for the first time. The waiting room was small with half a dozen wooden arm chairs scattered about. Louis noticed there were no windows, and he felt squeezed in and depressed by the dark, heavy room. Informed that the doctor would be delayed, Louis settled in for a long wait, but after only a few minutes, a short, dark-skinned man in a white lab coat hurried in.

Showing Louis into his office, Dr. Samad apologized for being late; he had used his lunch hour to check on an emergency patient. He appeared to be in his mid-thirties, and he spoke with a heavy accent that Louis learned later was Pakistani. He was friendly and did his best to make Louis feel at ease. Then, after poking and prodding him all over, he strapped a gray blood pressure cuff to Louis's arm. Squeezing the bulb until Louis thought his arm would come off, the doctor adjusted his stethoscope and listened intently. As he let the air escape, Dr. Samad's forehead wrinkled. Asking Louis to take three deep breaths, he rechecked his blood pressure. Then he unstrapped the cuff and said quietly but tensely: "Reverend, your blood pressure is 240/140 — the highest I've ever heard of!" He shook his head. "You need to get into the hospital right away."

Immediately Louis felt a stab of fear, recalling that his father had died at 43 of a cerebral hemorrhage. His mind raced. Will I die that way, too? Was that twinge yesterday the forerunner of a cerebral hemorrhage? Those things did tend to run in families, and there is no cure for them.

Coming back to the present, he told Dr. Samad that he would enter the hospital that afternoon. Slowly he left the office, feeling profoundly depressed, but determining to handle this crisis like every other one he had faced in his life and ministry: he would stay calm and not let this thing get to him.

Louis prided himself in being able to handle anything that came along. Which was a good thing, he reasoned, people looked to him for a sense of peace and security. He had to be the oak that others could lean on or take shelter under. Besides, he was not the emotional type. It was those tense, uptight types who got heart attacks. He was the one who could hold himself together, when everyone around him was falling apart. So Louis stuffed his fear and anxiety and all thoughts of his father's death into his subconscious, just the way he would soon pack a suitcase for the hospital.

When he arrived home, Dot was waiting for the report. Matter-of-factly he told her that his blood pressure was 240/140, and that he would have to go to the hospital. But to his surprise, his customarily unflappable tone of voice began to waver. He quickly got it under control — but not before Dot started crying. They both fell into each other's arms and held each other for a long time.

It didn't take long for Louis to pack a pair of pajamas, a robe and slippers, and his shaving kit in an overnight bag. Dot went with him, as they drove the five miles to the hospital. He had visited that hospital hundreds of times over the past 13 years, as two or three times a week he would go there to comfort members of his congregation who were patients there. He thought then, of the many times when he had comforted relatives who had seen family members die there. And he recalled visiting new mothers and viewing babies only an hour old. Most of the hospital staff knew him well enough to kid him — and now it was his turn.

That was hard to get used to, for Louis had never been sick a day in his life. Indeed, the only time he had ever been a patient in a hospital was when he was three and had his tonsils out. He took pride — quiet pride, for everything about Louis was low key — in the physical shape in which he kept himself. And he *was* well conditioned; I could attest to that, for whenever we played tennis, I would be gasping for breath at the end of a long rally, while he never popped a sweat.

But now this had happened to him, and I could tell how shocked he was, when he called me that afternoon, just before going into the hospital. "Bill, I've got to admit its got me scared; I'm not sure whether I'll make it."

"Well, Louis," I replied, "you know Who's walking through the valley with you. I'll be praying for you — and I mean that; I'm not just saying it to make us both feel good. And don't worry about your not making it; I'm not," I said as confidently as I could. But when I hung up, I realized that I was as shaken as my friend.

After filling out the necessary forms at the admitting counter, Louis was assigned a semi-private room on the second floor. Dot went with him up to his room, helped him put his things away, and sat beside his bed, until it started to get dark outside. It was five o'clock, and she had to go home, to get dinner for their three children.

As soon as she left, Louis felt more alone than he ever had, and now all the emotions which he had stuffed down, erupted to the surface. Fear washed over him in waves. What if he died? What would happen to his wife and three children? What was the matter with him, anyway? Only 37, and he was falling apart! His anger and frustration was followed by a rising tide of self-pity. He felt rejected, because he was not healthy, and completely abandoned by everyone, including God. Nothing good would ever happen to him again.

Then he searched his mind to find out what he might have done to bring on this terrible thing. Maybe, if he could find a sin that was at the root of it, he could repent of it and ask God's forgiveness and be healed. (I had to smile, as he later recounted going through these phases, for they exactly corresponded to the classic progression of someone facing a major physical trauma — Denial, Anger, Self-Pity, Bargaining, and Acceptance.)

As Louis tried to figure out why it had happened to him, and what he could do to persuade God to help him, he had to admit that for some reason he could not fathom, he felt guilty; he thought he had done everything possible to prevent this. He'd kept his weight down, gotten regular, rigorous exercise. . . and then his thoughts went back again to his father. Louis was 37; his father, an overweight alcoholic, had been 43. Only six years separated them. That thought alone was enough to keep him up most of the night.

In the morning, Dr. Samad gave Louis a heavy dose of Aldoril. Then he put Louis through practically every test he could think of. And every four hours, the nurse came in with the ubiquitous blood pressure cuff. The next day followed the same as the first, and the next day and the next, until Louis had been in the hospital for four days. All through that time, he felt like he was in a fog. He would try to push his way out of it and get free of the fuzziness in his head, but nothing worked. Several times, when he got up to use the bathroom during the night, he would start to lose consciousness and fall back against the bed. That was especially scary, for he had never blacked out before in his life.

By the end of the week, he was thoroughly frightened. When Dot called, and he tried to talk with her, his words were all jumbled — so jumbled, in fact, that the only word that came out right was the name Jesus. That really scared him! Here he was a preacher, who made his living by speaking in public. What if he could never talk straight again?

Louis plunged deeper into the pool of despair. No longer in control of his emotions, he cried easily, but usually when he was by himself. He continued to feel rejected by God, and had no desire to read or even watch television. He just stared out the window, while the powerful, icy grip of fear continued to close around his entrails.

Wednesday morning, Dr. Samad arrived at Louis's bedside and seemed unusually bright and chipper. "Reverend," he announced, beaming, "we think we finally have a diagnosis: you have malignant hypertension." He went on to say that they had caught the near-fatal condition just in the nick of time, and that medication would control the high blood pressure.

Instead of being grateful and relieved at this news, Louis was immediately bothered by the word "malignant", which he had never heard used in any positive way. Usually it meant cancerous and implied that whatever the condition was, it would soon get worse and was probably fatal. But typically, he kept these dark suspicions to himself.

Two days later, the doctor reported that, as a result of the medication, his blood pressure had been reduced to 160/110. Nevertheless, his grave manner when he told Louis his new reading, only added to his depression and pushed him further down into the hole he had dug for himself.

That same afternoon, Louis was surprised by a visit from one of the elders of the church. After the usual attempts at cheery, superficial conversation, the elder handed Louis a piece of paper on which was written a verse of Scripture. Haltingly, the elder said that God had given him the verse to give to his pastor. Obviously, such direct transmission of words from God was strange to that simple man, and he hardly knew what to do with it. But now that he had delivered his message, he seemed relieved, as if he had discharged some awesome duty, and soon made an excuse to leave.

Louis focused on the words. They were from the prophet, Jeremiah: "I will restore health to you, and I will heal your wounds."

Tears came to his eyes. God did care! For the first time since he had felt the twinge in his head, Louis found a ray of sunlight piercing his gloom. Maybe there *would* be healing for his damaged body! That flicker of hope within him struggled to stay alive in the midst of his suffocating self-pity and despair.

Louis asked for, and was granted, permission to go home on Sunday — one week to the day since he had been stricken at the church. Dot arrived to bundle him up, pack away his few clothes and the many get well cards he had received, and drive him home. It all felt so strange — this was Sunday; he should be in church, preaching. Instead, he was in slippers and old pants, looking like an invalid. As they drove past the church on the way home that afternoon, he started to weep silently. How would the church go without him? Would he ever be able to stand behind that marble pulpit again and preach the word of God? The doors were closed tightly and locked; it looked empty and forlorn. He felt the same way.

Recovering at home was not easy for Louis, who moped around the house with a hang-dog look. Nothing interested him; nothing broke through the walls of despair. When he spoke, it was as if doomsday had arrived, and he was its principle victim. He had no interest in reading, which he had always loved, and he fell asleep in the middle of conversations. And every four hours, Dot checked his blood pressure. Louis felt tied to that gray cuff and hated it, but he felt panicked without it. Each day, he swallowed a total of 14 pills, and they became a lifeline for him. With them, he could hold off the rampaging hordes of death that sought to devour him.

After several days of unbroken gloom and doom, Dot had had it. "Louis," she exclaimed, "you need to give up feeling so blasted sorry for yourself! It's making me sick! And frankly, I think it's keeping you sick. You need to be grateful you're alive. God spared you from a brush with death."

Louis frowned; this was hardly what he wanted to hear. From her, he expected sympathy and understanding. Speaking out like that was new for Dot. Whenever she had occasionally attempted it in the past, he had ignored her and responded with icy silence. Very quickly she had given up and not bothered him again.

But now, knowing in her heart that her husband's self-pity was consuming him and preventing any recovery, she rebuked him for his attitude several times each day. Tough love was the only antidote for the pernicious self-pity which was poisoning his system. And so, every time he would slide back into the slough of despond, with strong words of truth, she would pull him back out. And gradually, though he didn't like being deprived of her sympathy, Louis recognized that his wife's doses of truth were the medicine that was improving his attitude. That was probably what the Apostle Paul meant by speaking the truth in love, he thought — some love!

Regular visits to Dr. Samad's office continued, as Louis eased back into a regular work schedule. But there were restrictions he had to obey: no lifting, no strenuous exercise, and no pushing himself. Is this the way it will be the rest of my life, he wondered; I'm too young to live this way.

Probably the hardest thing about the new regime was having to ask others for help. He had to express his needs, and then let others do things for him — something he had never done before. But he knew he had no choice, for he was still breathless and deeply fatigued. And he was not going to be foolhardy enough to take chances. For the doctor had carefully explained what a near thing his trauma had been, and how close death had come. One single blood vessel had contracted and shut off the flow of blood to his brain; that was the twinge he had felt. Had it continued only a few moments longer, and he would have died or been permanently brain-damaged. In fact, the doctors were amazed that there had been no serious after-effects.

But that didn't make his abrupt dependency on others any easier. He had been forced to become totally self-reliant at an early age, had subsequently been that way all his life, and infinitely preferred it to his present circumstances. Louis had grown up in a broken family. When he was seven, his mother had divorced his alcoholic, unpredictable father. Before that, the unspoken family rule was that when his father came home drunk, everyone was very quiet and stayed out of his way, or his drunken wrath would take its toll. Many times Louis barely escaped a beating by being absolutely quiet and keeping everything he was feeling inside.

After the divorce, which Louis found extremely painful, he went to live with his aunt and uncle, until his mother remarried three years later. He didn't get on very well with his stepfather, so he began to find excuses to stay away from his home as much as possible. Soon he was living on his own, and coming home for meals and bed only. As he learned to adapt and fend for himself, his independence and self-reliance continued to develop. All the way through college and seminary he was on his own, also working 20 or 30 hours a week to provide for himself. By the time he entered the ministry, he was totally self-reliant — and proud of it.

But now all that would have to change — and that was part of his healing he hadn't counted on. But as he thought and prayed about it, he came to see that he really had not been relying on Jesus, nearly as much as he should have been; indeed, he had even counseled others that those who were admittedly weak, and who therefore leaned on Christ for their strength, were the strongest of all. He had preferred his own strength to the Lord's, and of his own volition would probably never have changed. Now that strength had been taken away from him — by a loving Father, who wanted His son to lean on Him.

There was something else he had to learn, another pattern that had to be changed: instead of tanking his feelings, he had to express them — his life literally depended on it. For the moment, he didn't have much choice about it, since he didn't seem to be able to keep his feelings in, even if he wanted to. But he knew that, as he got better, his pattern would be to grow more inward, and resume his oaken stance. And that could be murderous.

Dr. Samad may not have understood the spiritual principle involved, when he said, "Reverend, for now on, you're going to have to be talking about the things that bother you, anything, or the pressure of your pent-up feelings is going to drive your blood pressure right back up there," but he could not have been more accurate.

And Louis had already walked through the truth of that. For he had shared his deepest feelings with Dot — he'd hardly had any choice — and he had learned that he could trust someone else with his emotions. And that each time he tried to get in touch with his feelings and express them, he felt a lessening of the pressure inside.

After Dot, he began to trust a few others, myself included, and gradually he got used to the idea of being open and honest — with God, with himself, and with trusted Christian friends. Life settled into a stable routine for Louis over the next five years — restricted diet, 14 pills daily, reduced activity, periodic doctor's visits, and the ever-present blood pressure cuff. His pressure was holding steady at 140/90 which was within tolerance, but with no further lowering possible, according to Dr. Samad.

Then, in September, Louis heard of a new treatment, based on the elimination of food allergies. He arranged to go to Boston to get tested, and there he found that he had a severe allergic reaction to wheat, tomatoes, oranges, shell-fish, and a couple dozen other foods. The principle underlying the testing was that allergic reactions to foods can cause all kinds of other reactions — including raising the blood pressure. Once the allergenics were eliminated from the diet, the body would return to a normal, healthy condition. Louis started to eliminate those foods from his diet, and to daily rotate the foods he could eat — so as not to eat the same thing twice in less than four days.

Like everything else he had had to do, it was extremely difficult, at first, especially going to church dinners and receptions. He would look over a buffet table, spread with all sorts of pastries and baked goods, and realize that he could eat nothing there. His parishioners would urge him to try a little bit; one bite wouldn't hurt him, they said.

But he stuck to his disciplined regime. And the reward for his obedience: in two weeks, his blood pressure fell to 120/70! Gradually, with his doctor's permission, he reduced his pill intake one at a time, until within three months, he had eliminated all medication. At the same time, he gradually — very gradually — started to resume exercising regularly, until he had built up to jogging for 45 minutes each day. The side effects of the medicine — fatigue and mild depression — left him. The day came when he realized that his health had been fully restored — no, it was better than restored; it was far better than it had ever been before. He had felt okay before it had all happened, but now he felt — wonderful, that was the only word for it.

Just last month I played tennis with Louis. As usual, we were very competitive and went all out for every point, and as he usually did, he beat me. But afterwards, standing at the net, we both reflected on what a joy it was that he was able to play at all. I told him the truth: I had never seen him look better. And spontaneously, with great enthusiasm and oblivious to any strangers within earshot, we both gave thanks to God.

11
LIN

If we were God, we would never plan our lives the way He does — and would never be as happy, as we think we would....

"Please, Lord Jesus, if you let Jessie live, I will do whatever you ask me to do. Please, Jesus, please!" In desperation, Lin found herself begging the Lord to spare her daughter, as she paced up and down the waiting room outside the emergency room of Children's Hospital in Boston. Lin's first-born daughter was ten months old, and for the past week she had been feeling poorly, with daily high temperatures of 104°. Every other day Lin had taken her to the pediatrician, who believed it to be no more than a a cold or the normal virus that was going around the area. A little penicillin would do the trick, he had thought.

But nothing changed, nothing improved, and on the seventh night of her illness, Jessie was acting strangely. Lin noticed that she was especially hot and listless, but what really scared her was that Jessie's eyes were not focusing, and she was delirious. All night, Lin had held her in her arms, waiting for the doctor's office to open the next day. The situation seemed grave, and she felt desperate, at the end of her rope. For what seemed like the first time in her life, she didn't know what to do. It was such a helpless feeling, and always before, she had prided herself on her ability to stay calm. Now she felt sheer, cold, panic. Right at 9 a.m. she called and was told to come in immediately. She bundled her daughter up to protect her from the cold and quickly drove to the office.

The pediatrician's office was a bright and cheerful place, with scaled down couches placed all around the walls. In the corners were play areas for the children, and windows on three sides let in much light, adding to the good feeling about the room. But Lin was hardly receptive to the waiting room's charms, as she bore her precious bundle to the receptionist's counter and checked in.

Soon a doctor entered who was a stranger to her, explaining that her regular pediatrician was off that day. The new doctor took a history of Jessie's illness, and then said, "I think we should have some tests done, right away." He instructed a nurse to perform the tests he wanted, and when they were completed, he reappeared, surveyed the results, and said: "Jessie is dehydrated by 20% of her body weight, and I have arranged for her to be admitted to Children's Hospital immediately." He said it so calmly that Lin at first missed the impact of it all. Then, recovering, she almost fell off her chair.

Seeing her shock, the doctor asked, "Can you manage? Would you like me to call your husband?" Lin shook her head. "I can do it," she said, and she wrapped Jessie up and took her to the car, to Children's Hospital, and to the Emergency area, where the doctor had called ahead.

Gently but swiftly, a nurse took Jessie, laid her in a waiting bed, and hooked her up to a prepared intravenous tube.

Now, as Lin paced, the dark thoughts of Jessie possibly dying, which had harassed her the previous week and which she had pushed out of her head, came flooding back. Lin quietly peeked around the curtain drawn around Jessie. She looked so pathetic; the bed was so large, and she was so small. It seemed unreal for that little child to be hooked up to an IV bottle, and she seemed so lifeless, as she lay there. Lin could hardly stand it, so she went back to her pacing in the waiting room.

There was a pay phone in the corner, and it reminded Lin to call her husband. She reached Michael, an architect, at his firm's office. She wasn't sure how he would respond; during the past week, he had seemed not to notice Jessie's condition, acting almost as if nothing was happening. Lin guessed that he was really scared also, but did not know what to do. Now, Michael seemed to take the news about Jessie's condition nonchalantly. "I'm busy now," he said, "but I think I will be able to check in later."

Now Lin felt truly alone. She couldn't even lean on her husband in her time of great need. She grew angry at him, at the same time realizing that her own attitude of self-sufficiency had given him the message that she didn't need him. But she had never let him, or anyone else know she was desperate. She was accustomed to handling life that way — tightening her lips and bearing up under everything that came along. Now, in her anger, she rationalized that she didn't need Michael anyway; there was nothing he could do to help.

Back and forth she paced, her eyes furtively searching the swinging doors to the emergency cubicles, for someone — a doctor or a nurse, anyone — to emerge, with some word about Jessie. But there was no one. When she could stand it no longer, she would quickly walk back behind those doors herself, and each time they seemed to be doing something to her, but there was no word.

It seemed like hours, and it was. The whole world had stopped for Lin. Nothing else mattered, except her daughter. On she paced, and prayed with every step,

"Lord Jesus, please let Jessie live. I'll do anything You want me to, if You'll just let her live." Sometimes all she could say was, "Lord Jesus, please."

Finally, after what seemed like an eternity, one doctor met Lin outside her daughter's room and said, "What we've been afraid of, is meningitis. She's not responding to anything." Lin sank to new depths of despair, thinking, we're losing her. She's going into another world. She's slipping away. And she saw herself holding onto Jessie's hand, but slowly losing her grip, while her daughter slowly floated away.

Abruptly, as she paced, Lin now saw irony in the situation. She worked just three doors away from where she was standing. For she was on the faculty of the Harvard Medical School, a full lecturer of biostatistics. I know a lot about medical statistics, but now my daughter is in there, and she's not just another statistic; they're battling for her life. And nothing in all my knowledge or in all my training can help her.

With that, she felt again the awful panic she had experienced in the doctor's office that morning. For the first time ever, she had come to the end of her own resources. Always before, she could study harder or work more, or concentrate all of her considerable intelligence, and she could master the situation. Now it overwhelmed her. "Please, Jesus, please." The prayer was all she could do, and it went on and on, as she paced.

All her life, Lin had been the master of every problem and had met every challenge. She was born of an aristocratic Taiwanese family. Her grandfather had earned a doctorate in education, while her grandmother was the first woman of her nation, ever to be educated abroad. Her father was a world-renowned psychiatrist, who had been educated at Harvard, practiced in his native country, and then, in response to urgent invitations, continued his work in the United States and Canada. Very early, Lin had learned that the one sure way for approval in her family and in the world was through education.

From the first time she entered school, she had no difficulty in leading her classes in every subject. When she was 15, her father accepted an appointment to direct a department of the World Health Organization in Geneva, Switzerland. Though he was in opposition to the prevailing government in Taiwan at the time, because of his impeccable professional credentials and worldwide reputation and the national honor that this appointment represented, he was allowed to accept it. Education and credentials, Lin concluded, could open any door in the world.

That first semester of school in Geneva was almost impossible for Lin. She was enrolled in the tenth grade of the English International School during the middle of the term — and beyond asking where the bathroom was, she did not know one word of English. After the first day, she came home in tears, telling her father, "I didn't know one word they said in class today. I felt so alone."

His heart went out to his daughter, and he said, "Show me your textbook, and maybe I can help you read it."

Quickly, she dug the book out of her briefcase and showed it to him. Opening it, he frowned at first — and then laughed heartily. "No wonder you can't read it! It's Chaucer's *Canterbury Tales*, and it's written in medieval English." He laughed again, shaking his head. "I've forgotten what a lot of this means myself!"

Thus encouraged by her father, Lin began borrowing the notebooks of other students — and memorizing them. Math and science were much easier, of course, as they involved mostly numbers and formulae, rather than words. One teacher gently warned her parents, "Don't be alarmed, if it turns out that Lin has to repeat the tenth grade. She's trying hard, but there's hardly any chance she can catch up enough to move up to grade eleven."

In Lin's mind, those words crashed on the floor like a medieval gauntlet, thrown down as a challenge. Well, she would pick up the gage! She poured herself more into study — three, four, five hours a night were not too much. The only diversion she allowed herself was an occasional outing for ice skating.

As the end of the term approached, the welcome words finally came: she would be allowed to advance with her class. She had won the tournament! And she looked forward to the next. That summer, her family lived in England, and Lin studied the language intensely for three months. And they would do this each summer, and each summer she did the same. The rest of the year, she continued to study with blue-flame ferocity, and now, in Switzerland, as she had been in Taiwan, she was number one in her class, with a straight-A average. Initially, she had felt rejected at school, because her limited language ability; now that she had mastered English, she felt secure. She would be the third generation in her family to achieve academic excellence.

Her quest to be the best continued. Since her father would soon be moving to America, he suggested that she apply to at least two prestigious colleges in that country, and she dutifully obeyed, being accepted at both — Stanford University and at Wellesley College. She chose the latter, since her father had gone to college in nearby Boston, and her uncle was currently a student there, at Tufts University. She graduated with honors, majoring in math and minoring in chemistry. She then sailed through a Master's degree in public health at the University of Michigan, graduating first in her class, again with straight A's.

While at Wellesley, Lin had become friends with a Chinese girl, who had a brother at Harvard. She liked Michael and knew intuitively that they would probably marry one day, but she left him to pursue her degree at Michigan. Though raised as a Christian, Lin had made no personal commitment to her faith until she was 17, when she asked to be confirmed in the local Presbyterian Church in Geneva. During college, she had been too wrapped up in her studies to give any time to a meaningful relationship with God, and it wasn't until two graduate students in her department at Michigan invited her to attend some Bible studies, that she made a new commitment to follow Christ in her life.

After Lin had received her Master's degree, her schedule called for marriage. Now, where was Michael. . . . as it happened, he was back in Boston, finishing a Master's degree himself, in architecture at the Massachusetts Institute of Technology. She married Michael in May, and accepted a fellowship to attend Harvard to study for a doctorate in statistics. After three more years of study, again receiving all A's, Lin was granted their coveted Ph. D. Needless to say, she received a number of attractive offers, and accepted a position as a lecturer at the prestigious Harvard Medical School, teaching medical students. There, aside from being the only woman in her department, semester after semester her students gave glowing reviews of her ability as a teacher. She had finally achieved the acme of academic success.

But now, Lin, standing at the summit of the mountain she had chosen to conquer, felt a gnawing sense of emptiness. She had felt it before — each time she graduated from another school, or received another award, in fact. Hardly waiting to bask in the glow of success, she had quickly moved on to the next challenge. For the next goal seemed to cover up the uneasy feeling she had, of being unfulfilled. But now, as she surveyed the horizon, there were no other peaks as high as the one she was standing on. With no more academic or professional mountains to climb, what could she do to feed her insatiable appetite for accomplishment and success? She had unknowingly created a monster, and now it demanded to be fed.

For Lin, her drive to the top was fueled by an iron control. She had disciplined herself very early in life; she knew what she had to do, and did it. She scheduled and planned everything. Each day was ordered to meet her goals. During all her years of learning, everything else had to fit in around her studies. She had vowed never to miss an assignment or a deadline, and she had kept that vow. She managed to control the circumstances around her so that everything conformed to serving her goal. Even dating and marrying Michael was fitted into her life's schedule.

It was no surprise then, that Lin's next goal was the birth of a child. She calculated the best time in her career to start her family, even researching the best time of year to carry a child and endure the inevitable bouts of morning sickness. She became pregnant as planned, and delivered Jessie exactly according to her computerized schedule. But she forgot to plan on being a mother.

Lin had never given much thought to being a mother, assuming that she would hire other people to care for her children. That was the way she had been raised, and it seemed to have worked well. Oh, she had learned what the physical requirements of motherhood were; she felt comfortable in that role — feed them, bathe them, diaper them, clothe them, and teach them. But what should she do when they cried? Should she pick them up or let them cry? How would she to relate to children? All her life she had related to adults. How was she to amuse children?

When Jessie was born, Lin took a 3-month leave of absence to care for her. About a week before she was due to return to her position at the medical school, she began to feel a great amount of conflict inside; she was not at all peaceful. She wanted to be a mother — but she wanted her career, too. She had arranged for a lady in her church to care for her daughter on the days she taught, but she remained distraught. Finally, as a compromise, she arranged to teach only part-time. But instead of bringing her peace, the new arrangement seemed to make her more troubled and insecure about being a mother. The woman who cared for Jessie seemed more relaxed and knew how to handle her better than Lin did. But there was something else, something deeper and more disturbing: for she believed that God, in His still, small voice, was telling her that the time had come for her to stop teaching entirely.

She could not bear the prospect of not working, achieving, accomplishing. Where would she derive her satisfaction from? What would feed her ego, fulfill her needs?

Her thoughts were interrupted by a summons over the PA system for Jessie's doctor. She went back to praying, "Please, Jesus, let Jessie live. I'll do whatever you ask of me."

More hours passed — practically the whole day, before the doctor emerged from the swinging doors of the emergency room and walked with a tired step over to where Lin was pacing. "We're sorry," he said, shaking his head, "we can't find what's wrong with your daughter. But at least she's stabilized. We want to keep her here a few days," he said, obviously frustrated at not having reached a diagnosis. "You can stay here with her all day, while she's here."

Lin accompanied her now sleeping child to the children's wing, where she had a small room to herself, fortunately with a crib to sleep in. She didn't look as small and helpless as she had downstairs, and the room was brightly painted, with teddy bears on the wall. They did little to allay Lin's fear, for she noted that all the children on that floor seemed to have leukemia. Did the doctors suspect that Jessie had leukemia, too? Lin remained as frightened as she had been downstairs waiting in the emergency room.

The days dragged by. Every morning at eight, Lin would arrive at Jessie's room; every evening at nine, she would quietly leave, careful not to wake the sleeping child. There was still no diagnosis, but slowly she seemed to gain more life. Lin's fears subsided, but the inner conflict remained: what did the Lord want her to do? Down deep inside, she knew — but was afraid to say it out loud, even to herself.

When Lin returned home after that awful day in the emergency ward, she was surprised by a phone call from Betsy at the Community of Jesus on Cape Cod. "How are you and Michael doing?"

Since Lin and Michael had first attended a retreat at Craigville Beach, led by Cay and Judy of the Community, Lin had felt drawn to the people she met there and the truth she heard. During the first year of their marriage, both of them had spent many weekends on the Cape, attending retreats or just living with families at the Community. For Lin, it was a place of peace and security. A number of families from around the country had moved there and bought homes near a retreat house that Cay and Judy had established. Even some of Lin and Michael's friends had moved down from Boston. The people worked at various secular jobs, but came together every morning for Communion, and shared many experiences of common life every week. The whole focus was on Jesus, and the Community people seemed remarkably free in living the Christian life. They seemed real and honest — and how Lin longed to be like them!

She felt drawn to the place, and no wonder — everyone seemed to accept her simply for who she was. They didn't care about her degrees; in fact, most of them didn't even know she had any. One day, sitting in the dining room of the retreat house, Lin noticed the profusion of orchids everywhere in the room. She was startled for a moment, and her mind flashed back to her childhood home in Taiwan. The dining room there, and even the entire house, was filled the same way with beautiful orchids. She felt very much at home.

It was about a year after her first retreat that Lin confided to the directors that she felt called to live at the Community. They cautioned her to do or say nothing about that to Michael, for God never called just one member of a family; if they were called to join the Community, God would speak to Michael, also. But it must be God, not Lin, and so she would have to be silent and patient on that subject.

Almost a year later, Michael surprised her by telling her he felt they were called to live at the Community. He asked her how she felt about it, and now she could tell him of what she had felt, the year before. After that, whenever they visited the Community for a weekend, they spent time looking for a house to buy. Only seven months before Jessie's illness, they had found a house, immediately made an offer, and had it accepted; they could take possession by the summer.

Now the phone call from Betsy reminded her of their future plans. When Betsy learned of Jessie's condition, she said "Why didn't you call us? We'll put her on prayer vigil right away."

After the call, Lin was convicted by Betsy's question. Why *hadn't* she called? Because, she realized, the

Community and their impending move there, represented more of a commitment to Jesus than she was prepared to make. For to move there would mean giving up her job, her mountain-climbing, her credentials, her plans, her control, her future and, most of all, herself. Betsy's call and surprise was surely the work of the Holy Spirit. It was God's trumpet call for surrender. The well-educated, well-bred, always-in-control professor had to make a choice.

For a long time, Lin had allowed her life to be segmented — one part for Jesus, other parts for family, job, and career. She was perfectly content to be thus divided, only the longer the division remained in her, the harder she became inside. Now she was fighting the cosmic battle for her life, for relinquishing control meant being reduced to nothingness. Yet to keep on her present course, she sensed, would mean losing all desire for Christ. She was at a crossroads — one that millions of Christians had arrived at before her. Jesus or self — those were her only choices.

At that moment of titanic struggle, Lin told me later, she felt a little crack open in her hard shell of self-protection. "That night, with Michael beside me, I consciously chose to submit myself to God, and to do His will," she recounted. "That meant giving up my position on the Harvard faculty. That meant moving our home to the Community." The battle ended that night; the surrender was signed, and Lin signed up to serve a new Leader for the rest of her life.

Soon after, Jessie's fever subsided, and Lin was allowed to bring her home. As she left the hospital, she still did not know the cause of her daughter's illness, but she was grateful to Jesus for giving Jessie — and herself — a new lease on life.

As soon as they got home, Lin joined Michael in packing

up all their belongings and moving to the Community. A few days later, they were on their way. It was scary for both of them, but especially for Lin. What would it be like to be totally without a job and career? Where would she find her security? The battle had been won, but she was feeling angry about having to fulfill her commitment.

As she settled in at the Community, she found that she was angry about everything. One day, while reaching down to pick up Jessie, her back went out, and in excruciating pain, she was forced to stay flat on her back for an entire month. Initially, she was frustrated and angry that this had happened to her. She had never had a back problem before. Why had God let this happen? Slowly she began to realize that somehow, all her anger over not having her own way in her life, had collected in her back. At the suggestion of an older member of the Community, she started keeping a journal of each thing that made her angry during the day. She began to talk about these, including telling Michael all the times she felt hurt by him. Gradually the back pain subsided, and she began to see just how much the pain was directly related to her stuffed-down anger. As Lin began to practice simple obedience in her new life on the Cape, "almost imperceptably I could feel myself changing," she recalled. "I began to feel my worth anchored in Christ, rather than in my degrees and achievements. Others accepted me as a fellow Christian, and I began to accept myself. Stripped of my lifelong security, I struggled with learning how to just be. And I began to relate to others without my degrees or going back into my shell of protection."

What about fulfillment? "Surprisingly, I began to find fulfillment in the everyday tasks — caring for children, changing diapers, cooking, and singing in the choir. And as I did, I found more and more peace inside."

Did she ever miss her former role? "No, because the

tumult within me has now ceased, and I have found a very precious jewel — Jesus. I can genuinely say I love my life as a mother to my young children, and a wife to my husband. It's been a long road, but the peace and fulfillment I am now experiencing is more real and precious to me than any of that mountain-climbing I used to do."

Let go and let God went the old saying; thinking of Lin's case, it struck me how easy it was to advise others to let go, and how hard it was to do so oneself. Yet look at the results. . . .

12

REBECCA

Remaining single, if God calls one to, can be a challenging and rewarding life....

Accepting ourselves for who we are and learning to be at peace with our circumstances is difficult for all of us. Rebecca had a special problem. She wanted to fit in and be accepted, but she was an American Indian, and she was single, and perhaps she was destined to remain that way. I had known her for many years, and she had shared with me her struggle to accept herself and her circumstances.

It was already dark that Tuesday evening on Cape Cod, as Rebecca pulled up in front of the large, white, clapboard Dutch Colonial house. With the engine shut off, it was suddenly very quiet, and through the car's open windows she could hear the water from the bay, surging against the stone breakwall at the mouth of the harbor. The house, a retreat center, overlooked the tiny fishing harbor, but it was too dark for Rebecca to appreciate the view. Not that she was in any mood to appreciate it, for she had been upset for a long time — finally reaching the point where she had called the directors of the retreat center to ask them for a counseling appointment that same evening. Then, with her boyfriend Peter, she had driven down to Rock Harbor from Boston, two hours away.

As they slowly got out of the car, she knew intuitively that they were taking a momentous step. Peter seemed to sense it, too, as he rang the bell. The door was answered by a smiling young woman who showed them into the living room, where they did not have long to wait before being joined by Cay Andersen and Judy Sorensen. Following some light conversation, Peter excused himself and said that he would wait outside. For it was Rebecca who was almost hysterical and desperate for counsel. Rebecca nodded gratefully, little dreaming that that would be the last time she would see him.

Rebecca was born a full-blooded Seneca Indian, on the Cattaraugus Indian Reservation, near Buffalo, New York. An only child, she became the object of her parents' love and attention, and the focus of all their hopes and dreams. She loved her parents and always tried to please them, especially her father whom she greatly respected. As for her Indian heritage, she was intensely proud of it, and would carry that pride with her, most of her life.

There was nothing unusual about being an Indian, as long as she was surrounded by Indians. When she went to high school, however, and noticed that there were few of her race there and hardly any of them were taking the courses necessary to enter college, she began to feel different from the majority, and somewhat ill at ease. It was while she was in high school that she started to date Joe. The romance lasted for two years, and during it Rebecca was not particularly conscious of her background — until the first day of school, after the Christmas vacation. Joe was nowhere around. Finally, after school she asked a teacher where he was, and was told that Joe's mother had enrolled him in another high school, because she didn't like her son dating an Indian.

Inwardly, Rebecca felt shocked and rejected — but only for a fleeting moment. She was angry at Joe's mother for what she had done, but when she told her parents about it, they laughed it off saying there were many other boys to date, and besides they had never really liked Joe anyway. But in Rebecca's own eyes, she was a rejected lover, and she indulged in a few days of self-pity and a feeling of martyrdom.

Her racial difference was beginning to dawn on Rebecca. Most of the time, she felt fine about herself, but every so often, especially in social situations, she felt like a misfit. The Indian youths on the reservation seemed hard in their spirit, while most of the white teenagers at school were softer — and more refined. Because of her race, every activity that Rebecca joined in school made her feel like she was forging a new path; often she discovered that she was the only non-white person in the group. The difference was making her feel like two different people — one at home, and one at school.

As proud as she was of her Indian heritage, at the same time, as she progressed in school, she found that her friends were nearly all white — and she enjoyed being accepted by them. But that made her feel like a traitor to her own kind, and she was harassed by such thoughts as: would her Indian friends feel she was rejecting them? Would they assume she thought they weren't good enough for her?

Rebecca's solution to such thoughts was to cover them with a whirl of social activity and good grades. She wouldn't let anything bother her and deadened herself to any negative feelings. It seemed to work, and so she made it a pattern for the next twenty years — but in so doing, she was sowing the seeds of her eventual emotional downfall.

As for dating, she continued to see white boys and knew in her heart that she wouldn't marry an Indian, even though it would probably hurt her father very deeply, if she didn't. But that was a bridge far in the future — she would cross it later. The main thing to concentrate on was getting into a good college and getting started in her chosen field of endeavor: food nutrition. For that profession, the best college in the east was Cornell, and her high school grades were good enough to gain her admission.

She studied hard, far above the Cayuga's waters, graduating in the top half of her class and commencing her internship in California. She completed her interning at Massachusetts General Hospital, where they were sufficiently impressed with her performance to offer her a permanent position. She was thrilled and accepted at once, for she considered Mass General the hospital of choice — so good, in fact, that she had been afraid to apply there, for fear of being turned down.

Now, as she sat in the living room of the retreat house and poured out her heart to the directors, nine years had passed. She had risen to become unit supervisor in the medical building and had pioneered a talk show on nutrition on a local radio station. She was a young urban professional who had already attained a considerable measure of success, and her Indian background had not prevented her from achieving her goals. All she needed now was a husband and a family, and she would fit perfectly into the environment she had chosen for herself — about as far as possible from the future she might have faced, had she stayed on the reservation. But now, despite all her accomplishments, her life was falling apart.

Two years after she had started her job, she met Peter. Living in an apartment adjacent to Copley Square, Rebecca attended nearby Trinity Church. One evening, at a Bible study for young adults, she met Peter, and he asked to take her home. Soon he asked her for dinner on

Easter Sunday, and a relationship developed which would last seven long years.

Peter was an attractive six-footer with a Master's degree in accounting who wanted to go into his own business. He appeared to be happy and treated Rebecca with kindness and gentlemanly respect. He seemed to be caring of others, and although he was seven years older, he was very attentive, calling often. Here was the husband she had been looking for, Rebecca thought. She wanted an engagement ring desperately, as she felt it would prove to everyone that she could get a man to love her, just like all her girlfriends. With him, she could start a home, raise a family, and present her parents with grandchildren.

But the relationship with Peter was rocky, to say the least. No engagement ring ever appeared. At times they became very close and enjoyed each other. On other occasions, Rebecca would get so frustrated at his lack of commitment to her that she would tell him she wanted to stop seeing him for a week or two. Peter would agree, but in a few days he would call, and they would get back together again.

During one such separation, Peter began attending a Bible study in another town, and he became interested in a girl there. When Rebecca heard of it, she was deeply hurt; how could a man who said he loved her get involved with another girl so quickly? The next time Peter came to the apartment that she shared with two other girls — a large, six-room flat in an old brick house, decorated in early Salvation Army — Rebecca treated him as if nothing had happened, for she hated confrontation and would do anything to avoid it.

But this evening there was no way of avoiding it, and finally she told him that she knew of the other girl. He readily acknowledged it — which only hurt Rebecca more. In flat, measured tones, she told him she could not even put into words how hurt she was. When he tried to be understanding, it infuriated her, and she shouted that she was not going to tolerate his lack of commitment any longer and was breaking off their relationship then and there. With a sigh, Peter agreed and left. But within two weeks Peter had called full of apologies, and their relationship began again.

After seven years of riding on that roller coaster, Rebecca was an emotional wreck. She developed symptoms of stress, often becoming lightheaded and dizzy. Sometimes she would catch herself staring blankly into space; at other times, she would experience hot or cold flashes. And often, for no apparent reason, she would start to tremble uncontrollably. What pain there was from the tension seemed to center in the back of her neck, and she became very fearful, when extra pressure came her way. Once, she had been confident of controlling any situation, but now she was losing her grip.

What would happen, she wondered, if she did fall apart? What if she could no longer hold all the parts of her life together? She feared that she might just drift entirely out of reality. And yet, the thought was tempting; it would certainly remove her from all the pain and pressure she felt. One thing was sure: she could not make the symptoms go away, no matter how hard she tried. She didn't know what to do; all she knew was that she was desperately tired of living the way she had been.

She had reached the end of her rope earlier that evening, when she had gotten home from work. Throwing herself across her bed, fearful and sobbing, she had cried out: "I've had it! I can't go on! I've got to get help!" So she called the retreat house on the Cape, where she had often found peace and wise counsel in the past, and begged for someone to help her. Just at that moment, Peter arrived at her apartment. "I don't care what you want to do," she informed him between sobs, "you're going to drive me to the Cape — now!" Perhaps realizing that her condition was at least in part his fault, Peter agreed.

Now, just sitting on the sofa in the living room of the retreat house, brought her some peace. Cay and Judy, apparently sensing that she was literally at the verge of a total emotional breakdown, suggested she stay overnight. Peter, relieved, headed back to Boston, and Rebecca headed for one of the guest rooms upstairs. Newly redecorated, the room was cheerful and spotlessly clean, and there were fresh flowers in a vase on the nightstand beside her bed. Outside the window, she could hear the waves lapping on the beach. Rock Harbor — safe harbor; she felt as if, after being storm-tossed for so long, she had found a haven, a safe and secure anchorage.

The next morning, Rebecca awoke with the sun streaming into her room; she raised the window and inhaled the fresh salt air. The bay was calm, almost like glass, and it stretched away before her, as far as the eye could see. The sight of it seemed to reassure her that she would indeed find a similar inner calm for her spirit. One thing she knew: she should not leave that day. So, after one of the young women who looked after the Rock Harbor retreat house had brought her a cup of coffee in the dining room, she called her supervisor at the hospital and asked him for two weeks' vacation, starting that day. He readily agreed, for she had the time coming and had an excellent record.

The next two weeks were spent mainly in resting and in doing simple chores — they had to be simple, because her nerves were so frayed that she could not cope with anything complicated. But following a simple daily schedule brought security and some order to the confusion inside her head. And in her quiet times, she began trying to hear the Lord. So upset had she been over the past several months, that God had seemed far distant — and silent.

Almost before Rebecca knew it, the two weeks had passed, and she found herself again sitting in the living room, where she had poured out her heart to Cay and Judy. Her bags were packed, but as she sat there, looking at the ever-changing bay framed in the big picture window, she started to cry. She knew she was not ready to face Peter, her future, or the world. And she sensed that God did not want her to leave. So she asked the directors, if she could stay on at the house for three months. They agreed that she was probably not ready to go back to the pressures of her life in Boston, and told her she could stay. She called her boss again, this time asking for a three-month leave of absence, which he granted, not wanting to lose her. Lastly, she wrote Peter and asked him to pray for her but not to contact her for that period, so she could concentrate on receiving God's healing.

The next three months were like being in the recovery room at the hospital. Cay and Judy felt Rebecca needed a simple structure for her life during that period. It would be undemanding, but she would need to follow it and be obedient to it. And she would also need to be constantly listening to what the Lord might say to her, for they felt that He wanted to show her what was making her so emotionally sick.

Each day, Rebecca followed the same routine — chapel, breakfast, dishes, housecleaning, gardening, lunch, prayer, rest, sewing, fellowship time, dinner, reading, crafts, and Compline. It never varied, and she was careful to follow the regimen faithfully.

Compline was a favorite for Rebecca. She looked forward to that brief service at the end of the day, when those at the retreat center would gather in the little two-pew chapel for prayer and scripture, "putting the church to bed," as the Anglican Church described it. One night in late November, it was windy and very cold. Bundling up against the biting wind, she walked quickly from the house to the chapel. After the usual scriptures and prayers, several of the religious sisters of the retreat house began to sing a song they believed the Lord had given them. Rebecca started to cry, almost as soon as they sang the first words:

> My Jesus, I long to be yours,
> Wholly yours...
> My Jesus, I long to be free
> From all that binds me
> From all that holds me
> From all that keeps me from You...

Rebecca later described to me, how she felt as she heard that song. "How those words pierced me, deep inside! Everything inside me responded with a loud *yes*! That was the desire of my heart — to be only His, to be free from all that was binding me and keeping me from Him." And she listened to that haunting refrain, the thought came to her that her chaotic relationship with Peter was one of the things that was keeping her most bound. Was that relationship, and all that it signified, so important to her that she would put it before anything else, even God? As if by way of confirmation, the next day when a visitor arrived at the retreat center, one of the children thoughtlessly introduced Rebecca as our "maiden aunt". Immediately she reacted in extreme hurt — and realized how unhealed she was, in the area of Peter, marriage, and family.

Peter now became a persistent thought in Rebecca's mind: what was happening to him? Was he seeing another girl? Did he think of her at all? What about her future and marriage? Whenever these thoughts would well up inside of her, she would feel the old symptoms of stress and anxiety. One day, she was talking with Cay and Judy about this problem, when they suggested that she discipline herself not to think of him, until the end of her recovery period. That sounded drastic to Rebecca, but she was beginning to feel better, much better in fact, and she would do anything not to put that healing in jeopardy.

So, with God's help, she started to battle her thoughts about Peter. She remembered the verse in the New Testament, about bringing into captivity all thoughts, to the obedience of Christ. She had never done that, but was willing to try. Whenever she began to think about Peter, she called out to Jesus for help and consciously chose to think about something else — usually about Him. And gradually, much to her amazement, she found that by the grace of God, she actually could control what she allowed her mind to dwell on. In the beginning the struggle was intense, and she had to battle her thoughts almost hourly. But it wasn't long before her spiritual muscles grew stronger, and the discipline produced results. The harassing thoughts receded and grew weaker, and she felt freer and more at peace.

Too soon, the three-month recovery period was drawing to a close. Physically and emotionally, Rebecca was healed; in fact, she felt better than she had in a long time. Her neck pain was gone. Her head was clear, and she felt alert to the world around her. However, she still carried a gnawing sense of anxiety within her, whenever she contemplated re-entering her former world in Boston. On the day before she was due to leave, she asked to meet again with Cay and Judy. She told them of her improvement, but also of her nagging fear about coping with her hectic former life.

After talking with her further, they suggested that she

prayerfully consider extending her stay for a year. She said that, while she anticipated no difficulty in getting an extension for her leave of absence from her job, she wondered what they thought of her seeing Peter again. They prayed and said that would have to be her decision, but they gently added that, since the vacillating relationship with him had almost destroyed her emotionally, it might be wise to let the healing continue during that time. She gulped; it was a difficult piece of counsel. But when she prayed, she knew it was from God, and she agreed. For by the difficulty she had with it, she saw that she was not fully recovered; part of her wanted to hold on to a relationship that had brought her to the point of a breakdown.

Back in her room after that meeting, Rebecca took her Bible and let the pages fall open. Suddenly her eyes focused on the words of Jeremiah 29: "For I know the plans I have for you, says the Lord, plans for welfare and not for evil, to give you a future and a hope." She read on, dazzled by the loving promise of God to her, at the moment when she needed it the most.

Life moved on in an orderly fashion, during the next six months. Rebecca's days were filled with the activities of a budding community of christian families that was growing up around the ministry of the retreat center. But the struggle about her future continued to war within her. Though she was surrounded with women her own age, some of them friends who felt called to become religious sisters, Rebecca did not feel she was similarly called. But she had to be certain, so in the chapel one evening, as she was spending an hour in intercessory prayer, she asked God to give her specific direction: *was* she called to be a sister? As she sat surrounded by absolute stillness, she experienced a strong inner conviction that she was called to a different life than that of a sister. She was excited and wanted to share that certainty — not because she didn't have a call to the sisterhood, but because she had heard so clearly from the Lord.

From that point on, the battle in Rebecca was centered not so much around Peter, but on the deeper question of what she *would* do with her life. She still clung to the idea of family and children. She wanted to be like everyone else, and to be married was to be as normal as everyone she knew. She was willing to let the relationship with Peter go, but perhaps God had someone else in mind for her. Also, she had always planned to develop her career and continue her success. So, what was this detour all about? Was God trying to say something else to her?

Six months of her year off went by quickly. Rebecca learned to survive the cold blasts of winter wind at the Cape. There was less snow at Rock Harbor, than she had experienced in Boston, but the wind was much stronger and always laden with moisture from the nearby bay. So the cold bit deeper. But, at last, it was May, and the trees and flowers were in full bloom. The Community was hosting a retreat at the Craigville Retreat Center, half an hour away, and during the opening session on Friday night, the battle for Rebecca's will reached a climax. The sisters were singing words from Mark's gospel: "If any man will come after me, let him deny himself, take up his cross, and follow me."

She knew what she had to do: unobtrusively she slipped to her knees beside her chair, and holding out her hands to give a gift, turned over her whole life to God. She surrendered her will to His. She gave over her plans for marriage, family, and career, in order to receive His plan for her. And even as she knelt, she felt a peace steal over her that she had never experienced before. At that moment, the various parts of her that had once threatened to break off and fly away came back together into one whole person, the perfect product of God's perfect creation.

The long process of healing which had started for Rebecca that dark August night over nine months before, was now completed. Oh, she would still need help from time to time, but she could now arise from her paralysis of fear and anxiety and stress and feel like a whole new person.

Soon after the retreat, Rebecca felt called to give up her position at the hospital, pack up her things, and move to the expanding Community, to live among her new friends. The final step in her struggle came almost a year later, as she was sitting in the chapel, taking her turn at intercessory prayer. She seemed to hear God calling her to accept a single life. She nodded and let go of the last vestige of hope in her heart for marriage. Then, bowing her head, she told the Lord that she would embrace His call on her life and trust Him for the future. My first encounter with Rebecca came after she made that decision. While on a clergy retreat, I saw her walking with a group of young children, who were playing and obviously enjoying being with her. At that same time, she was part of a counseling team that brought help to several young retreatants. In later years, we got to be friends, as she joined my wife Carol in presenting the 3D program across the country. When she stayed with us, she would tell me parts of her story, and I added it to my growing collection of remarkable instances of God's deep healing. For as I observed the stability of her emotions, and heard the wisdom of her counsel, there was no question that God had truly performed a miracle within her.

One night, as we were sitting in our living room, I asked Rebecca about her call. "I don't know why God calls some people to be single," she replied, "but He knows, and that's enough for me." She thought for a moment.

"Being single is not better than being married, any more than being married is better than being single. Each call is right, for the person who is called to it. And by now, I've certainly learned one thing: my worth and fulfillment do not depend on marriage and children."

I asked Rebecca then, about her emotional healing. Could she tell me any specifics that made it happen? She took a deep breath and hesitated for a moment, as though trying to recall something that was buried in a deep vault. Then she said, "I think, for me, it was the discipline and the obedience to it, that healed me, through the giving and wise counsel of the two women, whom I had so often turned to for help. Those disciplines, given to me by the Holy Spirit through them, were the steps of obedience through which I had to walk, in order for God's healing to take effect and ultimately bring me out of my life's destructive habit patterns." She smiled. "God did it, of course, but it was through that means. At the moment of my 'breakdown', I needed order and structure in my life. Then, too, I was living in an environment where I had to face my feelings. All the time growing up, and even in my relationship with Peter, I glossed over my feelings and hid them from others, but especially from myself. Now, I was encouraged to face them in Christ, and work through them. And as I did, I started to lose my habit of staring into space — which was really a mechanism to escape my feelings. And as I became more real, I became more of a person."

Last week, I saw Rebecca on a television show, talking about 3D and the value of good nutrition. She was confident, at peace, and glowing with a sense of fulfillment. She had indeed become a person, fully accepting herself, and free from the bondage of needing the acceptance of others. Instead of robbing her of a future, her decision to follow Christ and commit all to Him had freed her to become the whole person God had created her to be.

13

AMY

God has a purpose for death, even when it seems senseless....

Amy had just finished putting away the last of the canned goods on the pantry shelf, when she looked outside on that early winter Friday. She tried to remember how many consecutive overcast days they had had in Canton, Ohio, where she lived. She and her husband, Ted, who worked long hours as the manager of a local restaurant, had rented an apartment on the second floor of a modest house in a slowly deteriorating neighborhood. Having been married for three years, they were struggling to establish a family and save enough money to buy a house.

Amy had been busy all morning with the washing, vacuuming, grocery shopping, and taking care of their two-year-old son, Gino. They had waited for this baby for several years, and he had brought them all the joy they had hoped for. But at two, Gino had become a handful, climbing up and down the stairs to their living room, opening the closet doors in the bedrooms, and reaching up to pull things down on top of him. The apartment was comfortable, but unusual, with two bedrooms and the kitchen and bath on the second floor, and the living room up one flight of stairs. Amy could hardly keep up with her son, he was so active, and loved to investigate every inch of the apartment.

On this November day, however, he was not himself, seeming listless, with no energy. Amy took his temperature, and sure enough, the thermometer registered 103°. She gave him some baby aspirin and carefully laid him in his crib, and she waited with him, until he went to sleep easily. She loved his room, which she and Ted had so carefully fixed up when Gino was born. On the wall across from the crib, Amy had hung a huge picture of a rainbow, the symbol of God's promise to care, and directly above the crib was a mobile of five colorful little hot-air balloons, turning slowly in the air.

After lunch, Amy went in to see Gino, and though he was awake, he still had a fever. She checked again, and the temperature had dropped to 101°. Still worried, Amy called her pediatrician, Dr. Van Tilburg. Over the past two years, she had come to love and trust her doctor, so it was easy for her to explain to his nurse that Gino had a temperature all day, and she was concerned that he might have a cold or an ear infection. The nurse quickly checked with the doctor and suggested Amy bring Gino in to see the doctor that afternoon. "Perhaps he needs an antibiotic," the nurse suggested.

Amy carefully bundled Gino up, put him in the car and drove to her doctor's office. Gino didn't like doctors, and on the way he said, "Mommy, don't go to the doctor. He hurts me. Let's go to Grandma's house. She's nice."

"No, sweetie," she replied, "we need to go to the doctor. He's going to make you all better."

Soon she pulled up to the modern office building, where Dr. Van Tilburg practiced. Inside, she gave her name to the nurse at the reception desk, and sat in the large reception room, waiting to be called for an examination. There were six other mothers with children there, and Gino soon went into the playroom off the waiting area and became immersed in playing with toy trucks.

Amy was surprised when the nurse called her name after only 15 minutes. The office was so busy, she had expected to wait an hour. She took Gino into a small examining room and waited for the doctor. Soon he came and looked into Gino's ears, eyes and throat with a small, pencil-sized chrome flashlight. Then, putting the stethoscope to his ears, he touched the other end to Gino's chest in several places, while he breathed in and out. Speaking in a calm, reassuring voice, he said, "Amy, I think he has some sort of upper respiratory infection. We will give him some penicillin for several days and soon he'll be healthy again. Don't worry, all children go through this. Gino will be fine in a few days."

Reassured, Amy left the office, got in her car and pulled out of the parking lot. As she turned onto the street, her eye caught a homemade sign posted on the front lawn across from the office. It read, "Maranatha - Jesus is coming." She thought, "Yes, Jesus, you really are coming sometime," and promptly forgot the sign.

When she arrived home, she gave Gino the medicine the doctor had given her at the office, put him in his favorite pajamas — the ones with football players on them — and tucked him into his crib, for it was 5 PM and well past his nap time. She gently giving him a kiss, she whispered, "Don't worry, Jesus will take care of you," and waited for his eyes to close, as he drifted off.

With a sigh, Amy went down to the basement, put in a load of laundry, then climbed the three flights of stairs to their living room and collapsed into their overstuffed recliner, for a rest. She had had a long and emotionally exhausting day and immediately fell asleep. She arose in plenty of time to fix the loving dinner she had planned — pork chops, one of Ted's favorites. With them, she made home-fried potatoes and a special tomato and macaroni dish which he liked. All the time she worked, she heard her own words echoing in her mind, "Don't worry, Jesus will take care of you."

Amy had gone to church as a child and had attended catechism classes for religious instruction at the nearby Catholic parish. But when her parents stopped going, she stopped. After she was 14, she never went to church again. It wasn't until six years later, when she was living by herself, that some neighbor women talked to her about Jesus. After several weeks, she felt she wanted to invite Christ into her life, and did. She felt better, but nothing much happened to her that she could discover. It wasn't until she had married Ted and Gino had arrived, that she and her husband started going to a non-denominational church, not far from their house. They both liked the pastor, and the small congregation made them feel like it was a family. Now the commitment she had made several years before started stirring in her, and she made a deeper commitment — giving Christ control of her life. Her husband joined her in that commitment, and they were soon involved in a Bible study group, as well as other church activities. It was in this church that she was first introduced to 3D and began to apply the Scriptures of each 3D lesson in a practical way to her own life. As a result, Amy's faith grew and deepened.

Dinner was all ready, when Ted walked through the door, a little after 7:00. They relaxed, as they ate leisurely at the kitchen table. With Gino usually still up at this time, they rarely had this opportunity for uninterrupted conversation, and made the most of it. Amy told Ted about her taking Gino to the doctor, and about the doctor's assurance that everything would be fine in a day or two. After dinner, Amy went to Gino's room to get him up, for if she didn't get him up now, he would never sleep that night. Tiptoeing into the room which was now dark, she approached the crib. He looked so cute the way he was sleeping, that she quietly went back to the kitchen and said, "Ted, come and see how Gino is sleeping." They both walked very quietly back into the room. As Ted arrived at the crib, he looked closer and suddenly said with disbelief, "He doesn't look like he's breathing!" Amy listened and looked for a second, and confirmed her husband's words. Then she leaned over the crib side and touched him. He was stiff and cool. She started to scream.

Clinging to Ted now, she fought for breath between screams. She had heard about the condition of sudden infant death syndrome, but never dreamed such a thing could possibly happen to her child. She picked up Gino and quickly handed him to her husband, hoping he could do something, while she continued to cry hysterically. Ted held his son in his arms and tried to resuscitate him by blowing air into his mouth, alternating by rhythmically pressing on his little chest. Nothing happened.

After one particularly loud outburst of tears, Amy suddenly heard a voice calmly, but firmly, say, "He's with the Lord; he's with the Lord." It was so real that she thought someone had come into the house. Yet no one was there, except two crushed, weeping parents. Amid her tears, Amy realized she couldn't call on God to bring her son back. She pictured what it was like for Gino to be with God, and she didn't want to interrupt his entrance into heaven. She wanted him with God — but she wanted him with her, too. Yet somehow, at that moment, she realized that he was not coming back.

Coming out of her momentary dream, she raced into the kitchen and, grabbing the phone, managed to dial the operator. She sobbed into the phone that her son was dead. Finally, the operator was able to learn her address and dispatched a rescue squad who arrived in two minutes. She also asked the operator to call her pastor, Rev. Andrews.

Amy rushed back to the room, and falling to her knees, kept crying hysterically and pleading with God to do something. Ted continued to hold Gino, but now joined her in loud cries of despair and anguish.

Now becoming angry with the situation, and with God, for not doing anything, she grew uncontrollable and wanted to break every window in the room. Oddly, at that moment, she realized that breaking the windows would solve nothing. She knew she had a choice to destroy something, or call on God. "Either I would go crazy with hysteria, or I could reach out to God and accept what that voice had said," she later recalled. "I knew inside of me that the voice was either from God or an angel. So the choice was mine, and I saw it very clearly. I chose to call out for God, and for the moment, I felt better."

The rescue squad arrived and banged on the front door. Amy rushed down the two flights of stairs to let them in. They hurried up to the bedroom, and taking Gino from Ted's arms, placed him on the bed and gave him oxygen. They ushered Amy and Ted into the kitchen while they worked on the child for what seemed to Amy like an hour, but was only about ten minutes. Checking his vital signs, one paramedic started artificial respiration, while another hooked up an intravenous bottle to Gino's right foot. Another hooked him up to a heart monitor and gave him doses of sodium bicarbonate, while the team leader phoned the doctor on call at the emergency room and reported Gino's condition. They could not seem to put any breath back into that stiffened little body, which they finally took to the hospital. Amy and Ted could only stand, and embracing each other, weep from the depth of their beings.

Fortunately their pastor came over, having received the operator's call, and drove them to the hospital, as fast as possible. Amy entered the lobby of the emergency room first, and went to the desk to identify herself. She was in so much shock that she couldn't say her name straight. Her pastor intervened and helped the desk nurse fill out the form. While he was doing this, Amy spotted the clipboard on which the rescue squad had made its preliminary report. Standing out in bold print were the letters D.O.A. — which Amy knew stood for Dead on Arrival.

The reality of it all hit her: she would never see or hear Gino again. Though the emergency room staff worked for another 15 minutes, Amy fell into the absolute pit of despair. Again, that anger she had felt welled up within her. She felt like smashing anything she could find. It finally subsided, and she slumped back in the chair in the little cubicle where she had been told to wait. She herself felt drained of all life, numb to all around her, and not caring to live life a moment longer. Her pastor came in and said softly those words she had heard before, "Gino is gone. He's with the Lord now."

Slowly, painfully, she arose and dragged herself across the lobby, out the automatic sliding doors, and into the pastor's car. The pastor drove Ted and her through the rain-slick streets. The darkness outside the car met the inky darkness in their hearts.

Entering the tomb-like silence of their empty apartment, Amy slumped into the recliner, where she had peacefully napped only a few hours before. And now she began to be bombarded with unanswerable questions, coming like rockets sent to destroy her. What more could I have done? What did I do wrong? Did I lack faith? Would Gino still be alive, if I had believed more? For months before, one of Amy's acquaintances had scolded her for having taken Gino to the doctor, instead of praying for God to heal him alone. The battle in her mind was increasing in intensity to the point where she could hardly stand it. "If I had just held him in my arms, he wouldn't have stopped breathing," she moaned aloud. "Maybe I shouldn't have put him down for a nap."

On and on it went, with no let-up. The hysteria she had felt earlier in the evening now turned to a fear of craziness, as her mind was being torn apart with charges and counter charges.

Finally, in desperation Amy grabbed her Bible on the end table and asked God to give her some relief. She opened it at random, and her eye fell on Ecclesiastes 8:8. Rather dully she read, "No man has power to retain the spirit, or authority over the day of death. . . ." She read it again, this time very alert. "No man has power to retain the spirit, or authority over the day of death."

She couldn't believe what she saw! Was God saying she was not responsible for Gino's death? Was that out of her hands? Was there a plan for her baby's life, with a beginning and an ending? That was what His Word seemed to be saying. And for the first time, she began to feel release from the flood of accusations wracking her brain.

Searching the Scriptures now, her eyes went to the page on the left, where Chapter 7 began: "It is better to go to the house of mourning than to the house of feasting, for this is the end of all men. Sorrow is better than laughter, for by sadness of countenance the heart is made glad. The heart of the wise is in the house of mourning; but the heart of fools is in the house of mirth." What comfort came from those words! It was as if God himself was reassuring her.

She read further, in verse 14: "In the day of prosperity be joyful, and in the day of adversity consider; God has made the one as well as the other..."

As she read, Amy slowly felt a sense of peace begin to creep over her. She remembered Jesus' words to his disciples: "Peace I leave with you, my peace I give unto you...." She was experiencing that peace which passes understanding that the Apostle Paul talked about. She shared with Ted all she was experiencing and then slowly and painfully prepared for bed and for a fitful night's sleep.

On Monday, four days later, Amy and Ted's relatives and friends gathered at the large city cemetery for Gino's burial. They had a plot in the corner of the cemetery, near a tree on a slight rise. The little white casket seemed so small, surrounded by the large hole. The pastor read comforting Scriptures and said meaningful prayers, and then the service was over. Amy's mind kept going back to the last time she tucked Gino in bed — a scene that would stay with her forever, it seemed. As she turned and walked away from the grave, she leaned heavily on Ted's arm, quietly weeping. She still felt some peace, but she felt deep grief and hurt, too. As their car drove out of the entrance to the cemetery, she noticed the MacDonald's restaurant where she had taken Gino for lunch just a week before.

The days following Gino's burial dragged slowly by. Amy had no desire to do anything. Doing the simplest tasks took enormous energy, and fatigue was a constant companion, robbing her of what little energy she had. Sound sleep was difficult, because as she lay in bed, she kept hearing Gino's voice. Food was tasteless in her mouth. Some days, she just spent the day in bed.

Her mind was haunted by the image of Gino's face. Scenes of their life together continually flashed before her. And it did not ease with the passage of time; five weeks later, when she went to church the Sunday before

Christmas, she was suddenly confronted with the children's Christmas program. Onto the platform marched all the toddlers who were in Gino's Sunday school class. She couldn't bear it, and rushed out of the building. But it gave her a warning of what an ordeal Christmas would be, and that they dared not spend it in their apartment. So Amy and Ted visited their parents over the holidays.

The torment did not lessen with the coming of the new year. Seeing two-year-old boys on the street would trigger an attack of hysteria. Some of her girlfriends had children Gino's age, and she did her best to avoid them. Every time she heard a baby cry, something stabbed her inside. At her church sewing group, the young mothers frequently talked about their children, and Amy always felt a sharp pain in her heart when this happened. They tried to be sensitive to her hurt, but she was super sensitive, and her emotions had been rubbed raw.

Amy tried to run away from her hurting heart, pouring herself into helping other people, for as long as she was forced to think about someone else, it helped her not to think so constantly about Gino. In their apartment, she and Ted had changed Gino's room into a guest room, so they wouldn't be reminded as much of who lived there for two years. But it didn't help; afraid to stay home alone with her thoughts during the day, Amy found every excuse to be away.

Meanwhile, in his own way, Ted was struggling as much as Amy. He hid his grief more, working even longer hours at the restaurant, to numb out his sorrow. At home, with nothing to distract him, he cried all the time. Never one to let his feeling show, now he couldn't help it.

The months dragged on, and the bleak overcast of the January and February days mirrored the sky in Ted and Amy's hearts. They were suffering through the longest, darkest, hardest winter they had ever experienced. But somehow, during those awful months, verses of Scripture began to surface in Amy's memory, and she appreciated the comfort they brought. The summer before, she had enrolled in the 3D program at a Presbyterian Church in a nearby town. She had wanted to lose weight, and a part of 3D's weekly discipline was the learning of some verses from the Bible. She had never done that before and eagerly soaked up the verses and avidly read the daily Scripture passages and devotional material.

Now, just when she needed it most, many of those verses came back to her: "I will never leave you or forsake you. . . . Be still and know that I am God. Let not your heart be troubled, neither let it be afraid. . . . All discipline for the moment seems painful rather than pleasant, but later it yields the peaceful fruit of righteousness. . . . No testing has overtaken you except that which is common to man; but God is faithful, who will not allow you to be tempted above that you are able; but will with the temptation provide a way of escape. . . . In everything give thanks, for this is the will of God."

Now those words began to heal her heart. And gradually she came to believe that God did love her and had not abandoned her in her troubles. It was still a hard time, but she felt reassured by the Lord.

One March morning, Amy and Ted were sharing a late breakfast together, as Ted didn't need to go into work that day until noon. As Amy was outlining her plans for the day, Ted suggested that she schedule a checkup with her gynecologist. That was not the sort of thing Ted was usually concerned about, and impressed by his care, she determined to do as he suggested.

Picking up the phone, she dialed the doctor's office, expecting to make an appointment for April or May, for her doctor was very popular and very busy. Some patients had to wait three or four months for a checkup. Amy wasn't prepared for what happened. First, she got through on the first try; usually the phone was tied up, sometimes for an hour. Then, when she told the receptionist that she would like a physical exam and a pap smear, as it had been several years, the receptionist put her on hold. After a few moments, she came back: "Amy, can you come in today?"

"*Today?* Are you kidding?"

"Can you come at 4:00? Dr. Lawrence has a cancellation then, and he'd like to see you."

Arriving at the doctor's office that afternoon, Amy was impressed with all the activity. A number of nurses were behind the reception desk, ready to assist the eight doctors who ran the clinic. Though it was near the end of office hours, there were still a half dozen patients waiting to be called for an examination. After some time, Amy heard the nurse call her name. "The doctor will see you now."

She was shown into a small examining room, and she knew from experience what the procedure would be. When she was ready, the doctor entered, exchanged a cordial greeting and proceeded with an internal examination. After he finished, Amy got dressed and awaited his return. Soon he popped into the cubicle and said, "Amy, everything looks great. You'll hear from us about your pap smear. Plan to come back in a year."

Two days later, while Amy was in the kitchen doing the dishes, her phone rang. It was the receptionist at the clinic. "Amy, Dr. Lawrence would to talk to you about your pap smear; can you come in Monday morning?"

After making an appointment and hanging up the phone, Amy began to feel the same panic she had experienced when she went into Gino's room that night in November, four months before. But before the awful fear could totally possess her, she prayed and asked God to make everything okay, and busied herself around the house. The weekend dragged by, while with God's help, she fought off repeated bouts of fear.

Early on Monday afternoon, Shirley, a friend from church who had volunteered to go with her, picked Amy up and drove her to the clinic. This time, the waiting room was filled with patients, and the office phones were ringing off their hooks. Finally, Dr. Lawrence's nurse called Amy and seated her in his small office. It was not as large or sumptuous as she had thought it would be, but she smiled to see pictures of his family on a table behind his large and cluttered desk.

Dr. Lawrence came striding into the office, and quickly seated himself behind the desk. "Amy," he began, "your tests show that you have carcinoma in situ, with severe dysplasia."

She didn't understand a word he had just said. "Is that cancer?" she blurted out.

"Yes," he said uncomfortably, "your pap smear came back positive. You have cancer of the cervix."

He tried to ease her rising fear by matter-of-factly outlining the next steps she would have to take. There would be a biopsy immediately which would confirm the pap smear results, followed by a laser treatment the next week. Then she would have to wait for several months to see whether the treatment had worked.

Holding on to Shirley's arm to steady herself, Amy was so stunned she could hardly breathe. As soon as she was out of the clinic, she felt like she was about to start screaming. She thought, haven't I gone through enough? Wasn't losing my son all the grief I needed? It doesn't seem fair that I have to get cancer, too. What have I done to deserve this? What about my friends who don't seem to have any troubles at all?

Amy continued to cry that night. She shared what had

happened with Ted, and she tried to pray, but she could not shut off her tears. She was consumed with fear, convinced that she was going to die, and that it would be a painful death.

That night, after Ted had gone to sleep, Amy tossed and turned, trying to find some respite. Finally, though completely exhausted, she knew she was not going to be able sleep, so she slipped quietly out of bed and went into the living room, to the same old recliner which had seen so much of her grief. With a deep sigh, she prayed, "Lord, I don't understand all this. Please help me."

Amy later described to me her feelings then. "I didn't sit long in that chair, before I saw in my mind the way I had held Gino in my arms, when the doctor was examining him in his office. I had done that to protect him and calm his fears, and through this picture it was as though God was saying, *As you cared for your son, so will I care for you. No one and no thing will hurt you.* Then I heard the words, *You are filled with doubt and fear. I am not the author of either one.*"

"So I got down on my knees and confessed my doubt and fear, and told the Lord I was sorry. Almost immediately a verse came to my mind from Isaiah: 'Behold, I am the Lord your God that takes hold of your right hand and says do not fear, for I am with you.' Bill, such a peace swept over me then, that I knew in the depths of my being that I would be all right. I knew I could choose to rest in God's peace and not in my fear. I recalled that verse from Deuteronomy: 'as thy days, so shall thy strength be.' That was all I needed; it assured me I could go through this latest trauma and come out victorious, if I stood in God's strength and not my own."

The next day, Amy had the biopsy, and it confirmed her cancerous condition. A week later, she returned to the now-familiar doctor's office and had a laser treatment. And then she waited four long months.

By now it was summer in Ohio, and on the day of her checkup, it was hot and sticky. Ted went with her; he had been laid off from his job, but after all they had already been through, they were able to trust God to provide for them. Amy was shown into the same examining room she had been in before. Again Dr. Lawrence took a pap smear, and as she waited, the Deuteronomy verse returned: "As thy days, so shall thy strength be." She believed that was God, telling her she would not die of cancer.

And sure enough, this time Dr. Lawrence came back, he was beaming. "Amy, the test shows no cancer! We'll check it in the lab to be sure, but there is no trace that I can see!" And the lab soon confirmed the doctor's words.

I talked with Amy by phone almost a year after her last visit to Dr. Lawrence, and at the end of our conversation, asked her what she had learned. She paused and then said, "Looking back now over those terrible months, I can see it was a time of real growth for Ted and myself. We couldn't stay babies in our faith anymore and were forced to grow up, as Christians. Also, we were drawn together in our troubles in a way we had never been in our marriage. More than anything, we learned to trust God to meet our needs. We learned that He would *always* be there." She sighed, her voice breaking a little. "And we learned about our need of the body of Christ. When we were willing to let our needs show, our Christian friends rallied around. We learned that God *wants* us to be needy, and not proud. But most of all, we've learned to trust God *always*."

Was there anything else? Maybe something not specifically related to the tragedy of Gino's death?

Again, she thought about that, before replying. "You know, Bill, I think I've begun to realize what following

Christ means. I guess I didn't realize before, that it would include pain and suffering. But now I see that it was in the pain that I drew close to Jesus. You may have trouble believing this: I do myself, at times: but the experiences we have had have been invaluable. I wouldn't trade them now."

She went on to describe the opportunities she has had to share with others who have lost children or been called to walk through the valley of the shadow of death. She concluded the call by saying, "Whatever else happens to us, we know the truth of the words which came in those first awful moments when we found our son was dead. Like him, we, too, are — 'with the Lord'."

Just last month, another year after our previous conversation, Amy phoned again and jubilantly exclaimed, "Bill, guess what? We've had another child!"

She was simultaneously weepy and happy, and I rejoiced with her, at the same time. "Amy, that's wonderful! God is *good*! Tell me all about it."

So she filled me in: after Gino died, several friends had come to them and told them that they felt God had told them that Ted and Amy would be parents again — this time of a baby girl. When Amy had received the news of her cancer, as much as she wanted to believe that her friends had received a prophetic encouragement, she believed that further pregnancy was impossible. She struggled against her despair, but she felt trapped by her sickness, by her husband's unemployment, and her past grief. Then, one Sunday when she attended her Sunday school class, the teacher opened with a verse of scripture unrelated to the lesson, but which she felt was for someone in the class. She read from Isaiah 49: "Can a woman forget her sucking child, that she should not have compassion on the son in her womb? Yea, they may forget, but I will not forget you." That settled it for Amy. She accepted that as a promise from God, and she stood on it, as solid ground in the midst of the shifting sands of her wavering mind and emotions.

Exactly two years later, her faith was rewarded: Elizabeth was born to Amy and Ted. What a perfect final entry for her file — and for this book.

Epilogue

I yawned and stretched — it was finally done. I had been through all my files. Outside, the night was pitch black, and the lone standing lamp cast a pool of light over me and the file cabinet and the stacks of folders.

As the last act of moving, I had been sorting through my files, trying to figure out which I would take with me, into my new call. Yet these weren't manilla folders — they were friends. How could I leave friends behind? Shaking my head, I decided to take them all with me, and I started packing them into the few remaining cardboard boxes that had not already been filled.

And then I smiled, again lost in reverie. For I sensed the presence of God in the nearly empty office. *He* had gathered up all these lives, and He had His hand on each one. And there was life and healing, sweeping over them.

Tomorrow morning, I would be moving into my new call and place of service, at the Community of Jesus, on Cape Cod, where I would join the life which had done so much to give my ministry what depth it had had. I was excited. Though I did not know exactly what the future held in store for me there, it didn't matter — God was calling me, and He would go with me, just as He always had.

Carrying the last carton out into the hall, where the others were lined up against the wall, waiting for the movers in the morning, I managed to turn off the wall switch with my elbow. Then I lowered my burden and turned back to the now-darkened office. I thanked God, for all that He had accomplished in that room — and for the privilege of being an instrument, however imperfect, of His healing.